Don' FORGIVE

JUDITH GRAND PRE´ SMITH

Positive Purpose Press
Chicago

DON'T FIGHT, FORGIVE

An anti-violence poetry book with morals and messages for parents, teachers and children

Judith Grand Pre' Smith

Positive Purpose Press
© 2001 by Judith Grand Pre' Smith

Printed in the United States of America

ISBN: 0-9711291-O-X

ICCN: 2001 130773

COVER DESIGN   STEVE CARTER, JR.

ARTIST   CHERYL MARTIN PURNELL

EDITOR   MILDRED D. JOHNSON

TYPIST   ELOISE DOTSON

DESIGN GRAPHICS   BOREL GRAPHICS, INC.

TABLE OF CONTENTS

ACKNOWLEDGMENTS   ix, x

INTRODUCTION   xi, xii

CHAPTER I PEACE HAS PURPOSE   1
        Chapter Preview   3
        The ABC's Of Harmony   5
        Join Hearts and Hands   6
        Don't Delay Be Peaceful Today   7
        We've Got To Have Peace And Pride 8
        Turn Around and Cool Down 9,10
        1-2-3 Fight Nonviolently!   11
        Let's Talk Things Over   12
        Partners In Peace   13
        Handle A Problem   14,15
        Peace   16
        Step Aside and Compromise   17
        Cultivate Peace   18
        Take Time to Live and Forgive   19
        Walk With Love in A Garden of Peace   20
        Compromise Before Confrontation   21
        Counting 1-2-3 22
        There Is Power In Peace   23
        Be A Peace Builder   24
        Red Light! Green Light!   25
        Curb the Urge 26
        We Choose To Be Good And Other People Should   27
        Don't Force the Issue 28
        Learn To Obey the Easy Way 29,30
        Don't React On Impulse   31

CHAPTER II MORALS AND MESSAGES   33
        Chapter Preview   35,36
        Looking For A Reason?   37
        Check Yourself!   38
        You Can't Be Strong If You Are Wrong   39,40
        Let's Help Not Hurt Each Other   41
        Don't Curse Use A Positive Verse   42
        Take a Hint and Work on Your Temperament 43
        Share – Care- and- Be- Fair   44
        Use Your Head!   45

Act Like A Lady-Act like A Gentleman   46
Put Good Behavior 1st 47
Teasing Isn't Pleasing 48
Catch Yourself Doing the Right Thing!   49
It's Worth The Time; It's Worth The Effort   50
Check the Time - Check Yourself   51

CHAPTER III VALUES ARE VITAL   53
Chapter Preview   55,56
Ten Key Qualities   57
Respect Others-Respect Yourself   58
Compassion Should Be In Action   59
I Value You — You Value Me 60
All People Are Beautiful   61
Let's Celebrate The Differences   62
Everybody Counts - Everybody Matters   63
A Student's Code of Ethics   64
It's Always Good To Tell The Truth   65
Don't Hate When You Can Appreciate   66
Don't Hold A Grudge 67
Respect Is Recognizing Someone's Worth   68,69

CHAPTER IV PEOPLE, PLACES AND THINGS   71
Chapter Preview   73,74
Parents Make A World of Difference 75
Someone Is Waiting   76
The Critical Thinking Alphabet   77
Black Family 78
The Way To Really Fly Is By 79
Parents: You Have the Power and Influence 80
I Am Your Report Card   81
Get On The Train Of Achievement and Gain 82
You've Got A Real Friend   83
The Hood Is Your Neighborhood   84
Parents: Improve Your Home and Family Environment 85
Cultivate A Friendship   86
Get On The Ball and Be Practical! 87
Don't Lock Out Your Parents 88
Change Can Be Beautiful! 89
It Takes Teamwork   90,91
Work Together as a Family   92
Parents/Teachers: Invest in Your Student's Success   93
Pleasant People   94

vi

It's Never Too Late To Unite A Family   95
A Smile Is Always Worthwhile 96
Our Flag   97
Just Saying, "Thanks" 98
The A B C'S of A Good Teacher   99
Mood Meter   100
Parents: Touch Your Child's Tomorrow   101
Cornrows, Cornrows   102
Everyday in Your Neighborhood   103
Fathers Are Needed   104
Drugs Are Nasty Bugs 105
Parents: Motivate Your Child 106,107
Fathers Are Everywhere 108,109
Two Classmates   110
Dr. Martin Luther King   111
Parents: Take A Stand for Your Children   112
We Are A Community 113
Don't Take A Vacation from Reading 114
Dr. King - Dr. King   115

CHAPTER V BUILDING PRIDE INSIDE   117
Chapter Preview   119,120
Put To The Test It's Best To Relieve Stress   121
Don't Accept Excuses 122
W-I-N-N-E-R-S   123
Alphabet Tools For Building Self-esteem   124
A Student Is A Student   125
We've Got Pride Inside   126
Give Me.... And I'll Be Satisfied 127
To Get Over, Get Better   128
Building Self-confidence   129
I Am Special   130,131
Give Me P-R-I-D-E   132
I Am A Light to the World   133
We Must Be Better Students One And All   134
Make Your Goal the Honor Roll   135
I-Can-Make-It 136
The 3 Little "C's" Are A Part of Me 137
Building Blocks That Make a Better Student 138
Attendance Matters   139
Oh Give Me A School 140
I Can Be Anything I Want To Be   141
20 Cans of Success   142

Growing — Within   143

CHAPTER VI MATTERS OF THE HEART 145
        Chapter Preview   147,148
        My Words Have Wings   149
        Beat the Heat 150
        The Language of the Heart   151
        You Make Your Own World   152
        Points To Ponder   153
        A Healthy Heart Beats Love   154
        Thoughts on Life And Beyond 155
        The World   156
        So ... The Cycle Goes   157
        Together We Can Make A Better World 158

CREATIVE ACTIVITIES   159,160

CONCLUSION   161

ABOUT THE AUTHOR 163

-ACKNOWLEDGMENTS

Writing the book, 'Don't Fight, Forgive' was a labor of love. Each poem, moral, or message was written to promote harmony in the world, especially among children. I wrote this book to give parents and teachers a practical guide to teach children to become more compassionate and tolerant human beings. This book allows me to convey the message of non-violence through poetry.

The idea of this book came while taking the courses, Special Education '441' and '442' at Chicago State University. It was in these remarkable classes that I learned 'Classroom Management and Remedial Techniques for Children and Youth with Emotional/Behavioral Disorders.' Thomas F. Reilly, Ed. D. was the instructor of these wonderfully stimulating and innovative classes. Thank you for your humor, intellect, and unique style of teaching.

I would also like to thank my best friend, screenwriter, actress, and producer, Tina Andrews. Our friendship has been a journey well traveled and spent. Thank you for always having faith in my abilities and encouraging me to do great things.

Additionally, I want to thank my good friend and mentor, Karl A. Huff, Ed. D. for your endless support and assistance. Thanks for helping me with my computer skills and sharing my enthusiasm for this project.

I owe a great deal of gratitude to Cheryl Martin Purnell for being an artist, editor, advisor, coach, and friend. Thanks for giving me practical suggestions and sharing in my vision.

I would also like to thank my family for being patient and understanding as well as my childhood friends from the organization, "United Towards Success".

Lastly, I would like to thank all of the educators in the world who are struggling to make a difference with our next generation of learners. It is through you that a good deal of morals and manners are taught. Our children are not lost; they may need a new direction of hope.

INTRODUCTION

Violence is not the normal human condition; it is learned behavior that may be preventable. Violence in our schools and communities in the form of physical fighting, verbal aggression, or psychological intimidation have many educators, parents, and children living in fear. Killings, gangs and drugs, along with the access to weapons of destruction are serious factors that confront children and adults today. Because the frequency, rate, and duration of violent episodes appear to be increasing in the world, everyone is adversely affected.

Violence is infringing upon the health and safety of our children at home and in the school environment. Young minds are constantly bombarded with violent images in the form of entertainment. Graphic news coverage and reporting adds to this daily dose of violent scenes and events. In turn, many children perceive violence as normal behavior. Thus, when children have problems or conflicts, violence appears to be the best and only solution. Feelings of hate, revenge, racism, or inadequate anger management and coping skills can distort the thinking and reasoning capabilities of our youth as well and may influence them to become violent.

More alarmingly, there are countless numbers of children who are so consumed about being victims of violence that they may not develop to their fullest potential. Being in a state of worry or confusion, many children can't concentrate or learn in school. These children deserve to be in an atmosphere that is conducive to leaning. Those children who exhibit violent tendencies need to be identified so that interventions can be implemented. Violence in any form only stresses the need to address this growing problem.

The title of this book, " Don't Fight, Forgive" delivers a powerful statement in itself. In a few short words, there is a message of peace, love, and forgiveness. The purpose of this book is to teach anti-violence messages to promote better social and moral behavior in our youth. This book can be used as a guide to encourage equitable behavior and thinking and to further a feeling of peace and brotherhood. Each theme centered piece was written to emphasize important concepts like cooperation, respect, caring for others, helping not hurting, and learning to be a good member of society. There is a common thread of love and appreciation woven throughout to help connect the human spirit.

Parents can benefit from reading and using this book. To begin with, parents are a child's first teachers. They are in a critical position to influence their behavior. This book was designed for parents to simply read to or with their child anytime a moral lesson needs to be emphasized or to promote peaceful images. Parts of this book were written to support parents in the difficult role of parenting and to create a better home environment.

Teachers are essential in the lives of children, also. In addition to teaching academics, teachers must direct their students to respect others, use common sense, conduct themselves in non-violent ways, show compassion, honesty, and to act responsibly, among other character traits. To accomplish this feat, educators can use the poems, morals, or messages to counteract some of the violence present in the lives of their students and to teach vital lessons on living peacefully in the world.

Finally, children are the main focus of this book. Children are our most valuable resource. They need regular doses of praise, attention, encouragement, and guidance to grow into positive and productive human beings. The repetitive verses and rhymes presented in this book are geared to teach children morals and manners and to use non-violent ways of handling difficulties.

As a rule, children are often disciplined but are not given consistent or regular examples of living appropriately in society. Some children are not taught how to manage feelings of hate, anger, hostility, or resentment. This book is an attempt to change behavior and in turn change lives in the process. The poems are short, direct, and understandable to reinforce important principles on improving behavior at home, at school, and in the community.

Looking at the people, places, and things that dominate our life, world and affairs, the importance of an anti-violence program cannot be reiterated. Whether a parent, teacher, or child reads or utilizes the concepts present in this book, the picture of peace needs to be as vivid as the images of violence in the hearts and minds of everyone.

CHAPTER I.

PEACE
HAS PURPOSE

Chapter I can be used in a variety of ways. The prevailing concept here is to set a peaceful tone and project the importance of friendly relations between people.

* The first poem, ' The A, B, C'S of Harmony' use the letters of the alphabet to enlist key elements of getting along with others. This poem can serve as a guide to teach basic attributes about accepting people as they are and to highlight principles of behavior.

* Other poems such as, 'Don't Delay Be Peaceful Today', '1 -2-3 Fight Nonviolently' and 'Step Aside and Compromise' affirm the significance of releasing negative thoughts or feelings to promote a more peaceful attitude.

* In addition, 'Turn Around and Cool Down' and 'Handle A Problem' can be used in role playing to instruct students how to use peaceful measures in solving conflicts or disagreements.

* Poems like, 'Partners in Peace', 'Join Hearts and Hands' and 'Peace' can be used very effectively as choral readings during school assembly programs.

3

THE ABC'S OF HARMONY

The a b c's of Harmony are easy to learn.
The words to remember are patience, tolerance, and concern.
The a b c's of Harmony stress with each letter,
The need to get along and treat people better.

The a b c's I can use and follow today are:
A- Accepting people as they are may be the best way by far.
B-Being kind and compassionate, too, is the right thing for people to do.
C- Caring about the feelings of others connects us as sisters and brothers.
D-Doing more to promote peace and love is what the world needs more of.
E-Enjoying the beauty in someone's face is a tribute to the human race.
F-Following your head and also your heart is a good way for friendships to start.
G- Giving is the best gift to consider because it enriches the gift as well as the giver.
H-Helping not hurting is a good rule, to consider at home, and at school.
I-Inviting a difference in opinion and more can open up new avenues and doors.
J-Joining a club or group is good in promoting peace and brotherhood.
K-Keeping a secret or a promise, too, is as important for me as it is for you.
L-Living a decent, responsible life will help reduce some stresses and strife.
M-Making an effort to get along is as simple as choosing right over wrong.
N- Noticing when you need a time-out is like using personal space throughout.
O-Obtaining an education and staying in school will always be a useful tool.
P-Peacefully solving problems can make a relationship better for anyone's sake.
Q-Quickly releasing anger and hate will leave room to love and appreciate.
R-Responding to others in need is a good way to help them succeed.
S- Staying focused and being forgiving is a clear way to enjoy life and living.
T- Thinking before reacting is great because it cools the mind with this period of wait.
U-Uniting forces to get a job done is a worthwhile effort for everyone.
V- Vowing to be tolerant may tell, how getting along can work so well.
W- Working on controlling your temper can reduce the need to cry, whine, or whimper.
X-Examining your motives from the inside out is way to improve on matters in doubt.
Y-Yielding a good result from good intentions, is a trait worth the time to mention.
Z-Zeroing into what brings harmony to our homes, schools, and communities.

The a b c's of Harmony build a better world for you and me.
The a b c's of Harmony are as easy to learn as 123.

JOIN HEARTS AND HANDS

Join hearts and hands
Linking love across this land
Join hearts and hands
Linking love across this land

Join hearts and hands
In the morning or at night
When it's cloudy, sunny, or bright

Join hearts and hands
After dinner, at tea
Whenever the opportunity

Join hearts and hands
At a wedding or celebration
Across this city or nation

Join hearts and hands
At a party or funeral
During any time at all

Join hearts and hands
Whenever the chance or weather
As long as people are together

Join hearts and hands
At mealtimes or at school
You won't have to follow any rule

Join hearts and hands
Linking love across this land
Join hearts and hands
Linking love across this land

DON'T DELAY BE PEACEFUL TODAY

Don't delay be peaceful today
Don't delay be peaceful today

Be peaceful at home
Be peaceful at work
Control your temper
Don't act berserk

Be peaceful with your parents
Be peaceful with your friends
Being loving and kind
Has no end

Be peaceful with your teachers
Be peaceful with your kin
Show love and compassion
Over and over again

Be peaceful with the salesman
And the receptionist, too
Being peaceful and patient
Is important for me and you

Don't delay be peaceful today
Don't delay be peaceful today

WE'VE GOT TO HAVE PEACE AND PRIDE

We've got to have peace
We've got to have pride
We've got to have peace and pride
Peace and pride together

We've got to have peace
We've got to have pride
We've got to have peace and pride
Peace and pride together

We've got to think peace
We've got to think pride
We've got to think peace and pride
Peace and pride together

We've got to feel peace
We've got to feel pride
We've got to feel peace and pride
Peace and pride together

We've got to see peace
We've got to see pride
We've got to see peace and pride
Peace and pride together

We've got to make peace
We've got to make pride
We've got to make peace and pride
Peace and pride together

We've got to let peace
We've got to let pride
We've got to let peace and pride
Peace and pride work together

TURN AROUND AND COOL DOWN

Student 1: I'm angry and I'm mad because someone has been treating me bad.
Group: Turn around and cool down!

Student 2: I'm going to get back at that teacher who won't give me any slack.
Group: Turn around and cool down!

Student 3: I was getting ready to bust his head because of something stupid I heard he said.
Group: Turn around and cool down!

Student 4: One, two, three, I'm getting tired of them picking on me.
Group: Turn around and cool down!

Student 5: That boy was talking about my hair; I feel like pushing him out of his chair.
Group: Turn around and cool down!

Student 6: He said, "My braids aren't real. I'm going to get him back so he knows how it feels."
Group: Turn around and cool down!

Student 7: That girl is staring at me; I feel like kicking her on her sore knee.
Group: Turn around and cool down!

Student 8: That girl pushed me in line. I'm going to push her back next time.
Group: Turn around and cool down!

Student 9: I'm going to fight after school because I heard somebody called me a fool.
Group: Turn around and cool down!

Student 10: I'm going to beat him good for talking about what I could have done or should.
Group: Turn around and cool down!

Student 11: He must be crazy calling me lazy.
Group: Turn around and cool down!

Student 12: That girl is always talking smack behind my back.
Group: Turn around and cool down!

Student 13: I'm not taking any more mess from that silly little pest.
Group: Turn around and cool down!

Student 14: I heard he called me a name. I'm going to get back at him by calling him the same.
Group: Turn around and cool down!
       Turn around and cool down!

1-2-3 FIGHT NONVIOLENTLY!

You will always have problems and with others disagree-
But, 1-2-3
Fight nonviolently!

Fight for justice
Fight to be free
But, 1-2-3
Fight nonviolently!

Fight for the truth
And the power to be
But, 1-2-3
Fight nonviolently!

Fight for rights
And opportunities
But, 1-2-3
Fight nonviolently!

Fight for jobs
For you and me
But, 1-2-3
Fight nonviolently!

Fight for knowledge
Education is the key
But, 1-2-3
Fight nonviolently!

Fight for wisdom
For the common sense to see
But, 1-2-3
Fight nonviolently!

LET'S TALK THINGS OVER

Let's talk things over.
Let's designate a Speaker.
Let's designate a Listener.
Let's give and reciprocate.
Let's reciprocate and give.

Let's come together and:

> Discuss,
> Relate,
> Confide,
> Communicate,
> Debate,
> Invite,
> Settle,
> Forget,
> Share,
> Dissolve,
> Forgive,
> Apologize,
> Incorporate,
>   And,
> Resolve.

Let's talk things over and do anything and everything possible to keep the communication open, positive, and productive.

Let's work things out and do anything and everything possible to keep from hurting one another and resorting to violence.

PARTNERS IN PEACE

We are all Partners in Peace.
   Partners to Live.
   Partners to Give.
   Partners to Love.

We are all Partners in Peace.
   Partners to Understand.
   Partners to Tolerate.
   Partners to Share Experiences.

We are all Partners in Peace.
   Partners to Care.
   Partners to Show Compassion.
   Partners to Cooperate.

We are all Partners in Peace.
   Partners to Respect.
   Partners to Relate.
   Partners to Reason.

We are all Partners in Peace.
   Partners to Help.
   Partners to Heal.
   Partners to Harmonize.
   We are all Partners in Peace to:
      Live,
      Give,
      Love,
      Understand,
      Tolerate,
      Share Experiences,
      Care,
      Show Compassion,
      Cooperate,
      Respect,
      Relate,
      Reason,
      Help,
      Heal,
      And,
      Harmonize. And, most of all, we are all Partners in Peace when
      our heads and hearts unite in Love and Acceptance.

HANDLE A PROBLEM

Group: Learn to handle a problem before it handles you.
The most powerful force is a thoughtful and positive you!

Student 1: When a difficult problem comes your way,
Lift your spirits in a positive way.

Student 2: Let your mind become peaceful and still.
Rise above the problem and get calm and tranquil.

Group: Learn to handle a problem before it handles you.
The most powerful force is a thoughtful and positive you!

Student 3: Monitor your moods; it won't take long.
Measure how you react be it mild or strong.

Student 4: Take small steps to see things through.
Seek guidance and support and take the time to think, too.

Group: Learn to handle a problem before it handles you.
The most powerful force is a thoughtful and positive you!

Student 5: Empty your mind of negative things,
That can hold you down and clip your wings.

Student 6: Don't hate or feel resentful, too.
These negative forces can weigh on you.

Group: Learn to handle a problem before it handles you.
The most positive force is a thoughtful and positive you!

Student 7: Don't be afraid to admit you are wrong.
It takes courage and guts to turn your life around.

Student 8: Learn from your mistakes; there are lessons to be learned.
Take time to reflect on the knowledge you have earned.

Group: Learn to handle a problem before it handles you.
The most powerful force is a thoughtful and positive you!

Student 9:   Grow in awareness and work day and night.
                And realize that things will work out right.

Student 10: You will always have problems throughout your life.
                The key is to solve them without stress or strife.

Group: Learn to handle a problem before it handles you.
                The most powerful force is a thoughtful and positive you!

                Learn to handle a problem whatever you do.
                Stay open and receptive to new ideas, too!

Peace begins with me.
>   With me, with me, with me,
>   Peace begins with me.

Peace is a feeling born within.
Peace should be shared with family and friends.
Peaceful are my thoughts and actions, too.
Peaceful is the state for all to strive for and do.

Peace is the stillness in my heart.
Peace stays together not apart.
Peace is the joy I want to share.
Peace is the feeling that shows that I care.

Peace can be an agreement between all forces, too.
Peacefully we must live in all that we do.
Peaceful is my composure during times of stress.
Peace is the calmness put to the test.

Peace is the quiet that encircles and surrounds.
Peace is the hush, deeply profound.
Peace is pure sweet harmony.
Peace should be the goal for humanity.

Peace begins with me.
>   With me, with me, with me,
>   Peace begins with me!

STEP ASIDE AND COMPROMISE

Step aside and compromise
Compromise, compromise
Step aside and compromise
Compromise this way:

> A - Adapt to differences in thought and opinion
> B -Balance both sides
> C - Cooperate with others
> D -Depart from hostile situations
> E -Eliminate name calling
> F - Find positive things to say
> G -Give and take along the way
> H -Handle problems without fighting
> I - Ignore troublemakers
> J - Joke without ridicule
> K - Keep thinking positive
> L -Leave past conflicts alone
> M - Make concessions
> N - Negotiate topics and terms
> O - Omit nasty comments
> P - Practice being patient
> Q - Quit being critical
> R - Resort to peaceful measures
> S - Strike a common cord
> T - Take a time-out
> U - Utilize ways to control anger
> V - Value the feelings of others
> W - Withdraw from verbal or physical abuse
> X - Examine your motives and emotions
> Y - Yield to build better relationships
> Z - Zero into getting along

Step aside and compromise
Compromise, compromise
Step aside and compromise
These letters show the way!

CULTIVATE — PEACE

Cultivate Peace
Grow it like a flower
Basking in light
Hour after hour

Cultivate Peace
With loving care
And tenderness
Enough to share

Cultivate Peace
In what you say
To those around you
Everyday

Cultivate Peace
With a warm embrace
That radiates joy
Upon your face

Cultivate Peace
With a friendly smile
It will make your day
So good and worthwhile

Cultivate Peace
Plant a seed in your heart
And water it with Love
As each day starts

TAKE TIME TO LIVE AND FORGIVE

Take time to Live and Forgive
Live and forgive,
Live and forgive,
Take time to Live and Forgive
It's the best and only way!

Take time to show Care and Concern
Care and Concern,
Care and Concern,
Take time to show Care and Concern
It's the best and only way!

Take time to be Considerate and Kind
Considerate and Kind,
Considerate and Kind,
Take time to be Considerate and Kind
It's the best and only way!

Take time to show Compassion and Love
Compassion and Love,
Compassion and Love,
Take time to show Compassion and Love
It's the best and only way!

Take time to Live and Forgive
Show Care and Concern,
Be Considerate and Kind,
Show Compassion and Love
It's the best and only way!

Walk with Love
        In a garden
                Of Peace
Holding hands along the way
        Walk with Love
           In a garden
                Of Peace
Practice this everyday

Walk with Love
        In a garden
                Of Peace
Smiles will greet you gladly

Walk with Love
        In a garden
                Of Peace
You won't feel sad or badly

Walk with Love
        In a garden
                Of Peace
Feel uplifted and renewed

Walk with Love
        In a garden
                Of Peace
Join hearts whatever you do

Walk with Love
        In a garden
                Of Peace
And hate will melt away

Walk with Love
        In a garden
                Of Peace
The time to start is today!

COMPROMISE BEFORE CONFRONTATION

Compromise before confrontation
Adjust and agree, positively
Listen and think straight
Discuss and relate

Be sure to:
> Adapt,
> Accept,
> Settle,
> Make Concessions,
> Negotiate,
> Retreat,
> Accommodate,
> Reflect,
> Request,
> Bargain,
> Trade-off,
> Correlate,
> Assist,
> Contribute,
> Arbitrate,
> Temper,
> Collaborate,
> And,
> Reciprocate.

Try to do all of these things before you confront someone.
Take time to think, calm down, and cool-off.
Compromise before confrontation.
There is a better way to solve problems today!

COUNTING 1 -2 - 3

Counting 1-2-3, I will act Peacefully
                    I will act Peacefully
                    I will act Peacefully

Counting 1-2-3, I will act Peacefully
                    I will act Peacefully
Counting 1-2-3.

Saying a-b-c-, I will live Peacefully
                    I will live Peacefully
                    I will live Peacefully

Saying a-b-c, I will live Peacefully
                    I will live Peacefully
Saying a-b-c.

Singing do-re-mi, I will talk Peacefully
                    I will talk Peacefully
                    I will talk Peacefully

Singing do-re-mi, I will talk Peacefully
                    I will talk Peacefully
Singing do-re-mi.

Clapping 1-2-3, I will think Peacefully
                    I will think Peacefully
                    I will think Peacefully

Clapping 1-2-3, I will think Peacefully
                    I will think Peacefully
Clapping 1-2-3.

THERE IS POWER IN PEACE

There is Power in Peace
Peace has Power

It has the Power to Surround
It has Power, Profound

There is Power in Peace
Peace has Power

      It has the Power to Enlighten
      It has the Power to Brighten

There is Power in Peace
Peace has Power

      It has the Power to Harmonize
      It has the Power to Energize

There is Power in Peace
Peace has Power

      It has the Power to Instill
      It has the Power to Fill

There is Power in Peace
Peace has Power

      It has the Power to Thrive
      It has the Power to Survive

There is Power in Peace
Peace has Power

      It has the Power to Live
      It has the Power to Give

There is Power in Peace
Peace has Power

BE A PEACE BUILDER

Be a Peace Builder
And Build a Foundation of Peace.

Think about what you are doing.
Think about what you are saying.
Think about what you are thinking.

Build a bridge of Wholeness.
Build a bridge of Harmony.
Build a bridge of Peace.

Watch what you are doing.
Watch what you are saying.
Watch what you are thinking.

Be a Peace Builder
And Build a Foundation of Peace.

Respond to others without Anger.
Respond to others without Fighting.
Respond to others without Violence.

Think Peaceful Thoughts.
Think Positive Thoughts.
Think Productive Thoughts.

Surround your Negative Feelings in a Circle of Love.
Embrace Anger with Calm and Quiet.
Relax your Mind, Body, and Senses.
Step into a pool of refreshing waters and let go.

Be a Peace Builder
And Build a Foundation of Peace.

RED LIGHT! GREEN LIGHT!

Group: Red light! Green light! Stop, think and don't fight!
Student 1: Watch what you do and watch what you say. Think before you react each and everyday.

Group: Red light! Green light! Stop, think and don't fight!
Student 2: Get along with your classmates; get along with your friends. When conflicts occur, be flexible and bend.

Group: Red light! Green light! Stop, think and don't fight!
Student 3: Use kind words when talking to others. Look at people as your sisters and brothers.

Group: Red light! Green light! Stop, think and don't fight!
Student 4: Everyone is different. We all have a choice. You can't force others to agree with your opinion or voice.

Group: Red light! Green light! Stop, think and don't fight!
Student 5: If you can't get along with a friend or foe, give each other space and a place to go.

Group: Red light! Green light! Stop, think and don't fight!
Student 6: Every person has a story he wants to tell, the key is to show interest and listen well.

Group: Red light! Green light! Stop, think and don't fight!
Student 7: People are in this world to live and work together; no matter what the time, no matter what kind of weather.

Group: Red light! Green light! Stop, think and don't fight!
Student 8: During times of conflict, we all can be heard. Remember the slogan and repeat the words:

Group: Red light! Green light! Stop, think, and don't fight!

CURB THE URGE

Curb the urge
To slap and hit

Curb the urge
To throw a fit

Curb the urge
To yell and scream

Curb the urge
To do something mean

Curb the urge
To curse and shout

Curb the urge
To play and act-out

Curb the urge
To push and kick

Curb the urge
To pass some licks

Curb the urge
To laugh and joke

Curb the urge
To pinch and poke

Curb the urge
To scratch and fight

Curb the urge
And do something right!

WE CHOOSE TO BE GOOD AND OTHER PEOPLE SHOULD

Group: We choose to be good and other people should.

Girls: If we see someone cheating on a test, we choose to study and try to do our best.

Group: We choose to be good and other people should.

Boys: If we see people fighting or shouting something bad, we choose not to do that when we get angry or mad.

Group: We choose to be good and other people should.

Girls: If we see people pushing or shoving in line, we choose to let them know that they should be patient and kind.

Group: We choose to be good and other people should.

Boys: If we hear people making fun of someone, we choose to remind them that we are equal under the sun.

Group: We choose to be good and other people should.

Girls: If we hear people screaming or shouting really loud, we choose to remind them that they should act dignified and proud.

Group: We choose to be good and other people should.
We choose to be good and other people should.

DON'T FORCE THE ISSUE

When life gets confusing and the outlook seems bad,
Don't force the issue and get really mad!

If you want everything to go your way,
Don't force the issue and be angry today!

When everyone is wrong and you're the only one right,
Don't force the issue and get uptight!

If your folks don't agree with your every whim,
Don't force the issue and get hostile towards them!

When your parents won't listen to what you have to say,
Don't force the issue and turn away!

If friends don't know or understand,
Don't force the issue with the matters at hand!

When nobody is around to help you get going,
Don't force the issue; just keep things flowing!

LEARN TO OBEY THE EASY WAY

Group: There are various steps
        To keep in mind
        To obey well
        And stay in line

Student 1: Listen carefully
        Get quiet, don't shout
        Listen to what obeying
        Is all about

Group: Learn to obey the easy way
        The easy way is to always obey

Student 2: Listen to the directions
        Focus 1-2-3
        Remember things in order
        It won't be hard to see

Group: Learn to obey the easy way
        The easy way is to always obey

Student 3: Focus your attention
        On the task at hand
        Think and reason
        React on demand

Group: Learn to obey the easy way
        The easy way is to always obey

Student 4: Check the information
        Check on what you have to do
        It's really very simple
        To see things through

Group: Learn to obey the easy way
        The easy way is to always obey

Student 5: Don't talk back
        Do what you are told
        It's better to be obedient
        Than brazen and bold

Group: Learn to obey the easy way
       The easy way is to always obey

Student 6:   Obeying up front
              Will save a lot of time
              It should be done
              Without excuses or rhymes

Group: Learn to obey the easy way
       The easy way is to always obey

DON'T REACT ON IMPULSE

Don't react on impulse

Don't react on impulse

Don't react on impulse

Don't react on impulse

Don't react on impulse

Don't react on impulse

Don't react on impulse

Don't react on impulse

Don't react on impulse

Don't react on impulse

Don't react on impulse

Don't react on impulse

When others make you mad

If you're feeling down or sad

If someone calls you names

When playing cards or games

When things don't go your way

Remember this each day

Take time to think things through

Your response is up to you

Control your emotions now

Make a promise or a vow

Cool your temper down

Then, turn your life around

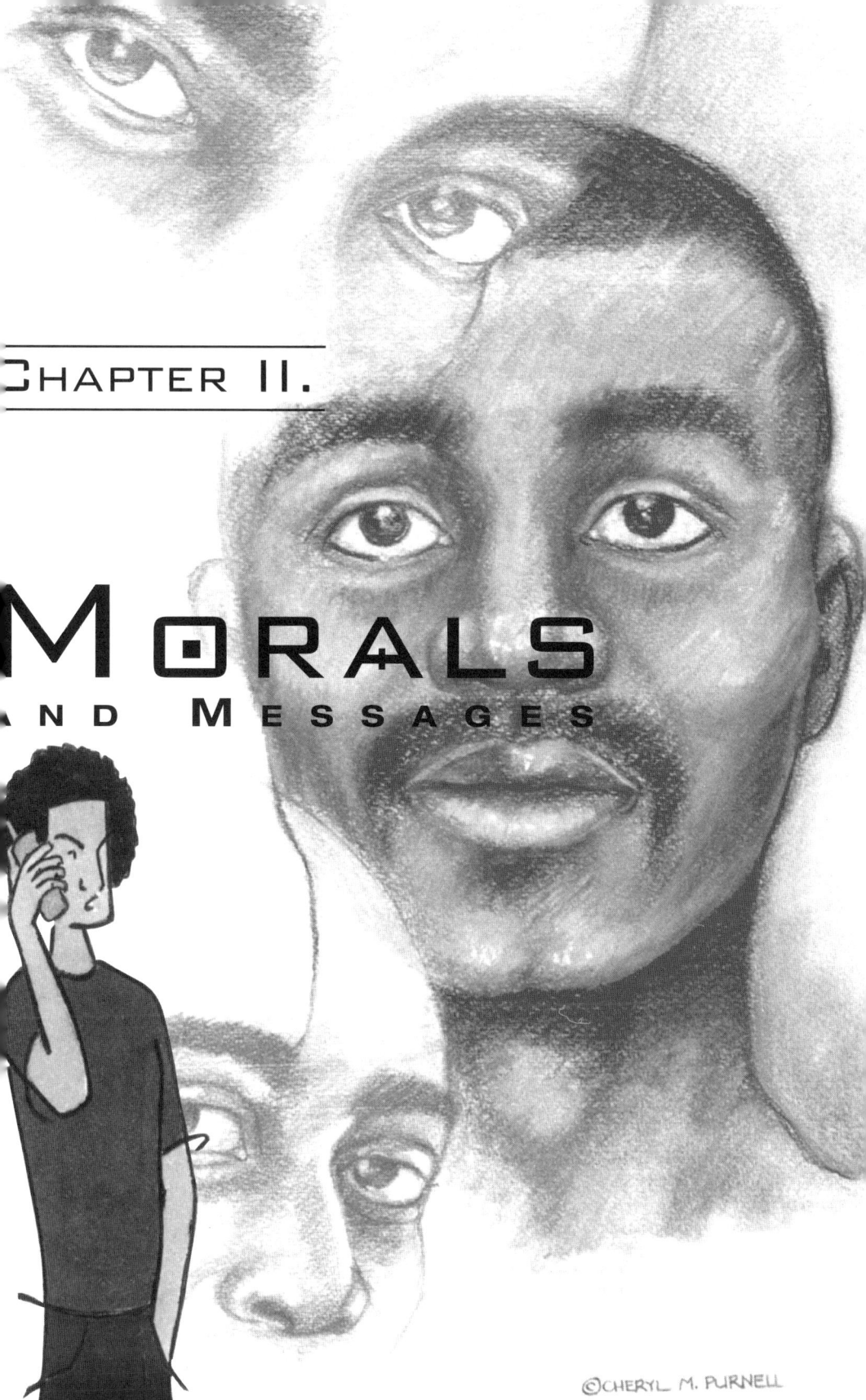

CHAPTER II.

MORALS
AND MESSAGES

©CHERYL M. PURNELL

Chapter II emphasizes basic social skills that

may need to be reinforced. Many poems in

this chapter examine how to conduct yourself

properly in different situations.

* Examples of this principal
  include, 'Check Yourself! ',
  'You Can't Be Strong If You
  Are Wrong', 'Lets Help Not
  Hurt Each Other', and '
  Don't Curse Use A Positive
  Verse'.

Children always need good models to follow especially when it

comes to acting appropriately in public.

* Poems like 'Share-Care-and
  Be-Fair', ' Use Your Head!'
  and 'Put Good Behavior 1st'
  teach this valuable concept.

Teasing is an annoying habit that should not be taken lightly.

* The poem 'Teasing Isn't
  Pleasing' was written to
  emphasize that teasing is
  wrong and can have
  devastating effects on some
  children. Similarly, the poem
  'Catch Yourself Doing the
  Right Thing' discusses the
  urgency of doing the right
  thing in the midst of negative
  actions.

Additionally, the selections entitled:

* 'Take a Hint and Work on

35

Your Temperament' and 'Act Like a Lady-Act Like a Gentleman' can make strong statements in demonstrating acceptable behavior at home, at school, and in the community.

This chapter can also be used to reinforce rules of

behavior when playing sports or games. It is always

a good idea for children to memorize and recite

these principles of conduct on a regular basis.

L-O-O-K-I-N-G F-O-R A R-E-A-S-O-N?

Are you looking for a reason to do something mean?
Are you looking for a reason to do something bad?
Are you looking for a reason to call someone names?
Are you looking for a reason to curse someone out?
Are you looking for a reason to beat someone up?
Are you looking for a reason to lie and cheat?
Are you looking for a reason to steal?
Are you looking for a reason to kill?
Are you looking for a reason to get revenge?
Are you looking for a reason to betray a trust?
Are you looking for a reason to fight?
Are you looking for a reason to disrespect your parents and teachers?
Are you looking for a reason to ridicule or antagonize?
Are you looking for a reason to criticize or belittle?
Are you looking for a reason to be nasty or hateful?
Are you looking for a reason to hurt someone?
There are endless reasons or excuses you can give to justify doing something mean, nasty, or hateful. But, there is only one reason to consider. If it sounds wrong, feels wrong, looks wrong, tastes wrong, or smells wrong, it is wrong!

It is always wrong to:
   1. Do something mean.
   2. Do something bad.
   3. Call someone names.
   4. Curse someone out.
   5. Beat someone up.
   6. Lie and cheat.
   7. Steal.
   8. Kill.
   9. Get revenge.
   10. Betray a trust.
   11. Start a fight.
   12. Disrespect your parents and teachers.
   13. Ridicule or antagonize.
   14. Criticize or belittle.
   15. Be nasty or hateful.
   16. Hurt someone in any way. Are you looking for a reason?
   Stop, Think, and Listen. It is always wrong to do something wrong.

CHECK YOURSELF!

When anger builds up
Like an overflowing cup
Check Yourself!
Check Yourself!

When hate starts brewing
And emotions are stewing
Check Yourself!
Check Yourself!

When things get hot
Like a boiling pot
Check Yourself!
Check Yourself!

When life gets rough
And the going gets tough
Check Yourself!
Check Yourself!

When tempers start to rise
Don't act surprised-
Check Yourself!
Check Yourself!

When you get mad
Things won't be so bad, if you
Check Yourself!
Check Yourself!

YOU CAN'T BE STRONG IF YOU ARE WRONG

You can't be strong if you are wrong
You can't be strong if you are wrong

You are wrong -
When you say bad words
Or act really wild like you are disturbed

You are wrong -
When you bully or fight
Or say, "Your mother"
That isn't right

You are wrong -
When you push in line
Or jump in front of others
Sometimes

You are wrong -
When you just don't care
About other's feelings
Here or there

You are wrong -
When you shout out loud
Or, act real ugly
Instead of proud

You are wrong -
When you hit or kick
At a boy or girl
That makes you sick

You are wrong -
When you fuss and cuss
Or make fun of someone
In a car or bus

You are wrong -
When you steal or lie
Or if you punch a person
In the eye

You are wrong -
When you treat someone bad
Or laugh or joke
If a person is feeling sad

You are wrong -
When you lose a game
And be a bad sport
By calling your opponents names

You are wrong -
When you hit or shove
Or think that hate
Is stronger than love

You can't be strong if you are wrong
You can't be strong if you are wrong

LET'S HELP NOT HURT EACH OTHER

Let's help not hurt each other
Let's help not hurt each other

Let's help not hurt
Each other, each other
Let's help not hurt each other

Help your mother
Help your father
Help your sister
Help your brother

Help your neighbor
Help your teacher
Help your classmates
Help your preacher

Help your aunt
Help your kin
Help your uncle
Help your friend

Let's help not hurt each other
Let's help not hurt each other

Let's help not hurt
Each other, each other
Let's help not hurt each other

DON'T CURSE USE A POSITIVE VERSE

Don't curse use a positive verse
Don't curse use a positive verse
Like:
> Love your neighbor
> Think right
> Share with others
> Don't fight

Don't curse use a positive verse
Don't curse use a positive verse
Like:
> Stop the violence
> Learn to live
> Peacefully-
> Be generous and give

Don't curse use a positive verse
Don't curse use a positive verse
Like:
> Don't talk about
> Anyone's mother
> We're all on this earth
> To help each other

Don't curse use a positive verse
Don't curse use a positive verse
Like:
> Respect your teachers
> Respect your friends
> Respect your parents
> Again and again

Don't curse use a positive verse
Don't curse use a positive verse
Like:
> Take time to do
> Something good
> Stay in school
> The way you should

Don't curse use a positive verse
Don't curse use a positive verse

TAKE A HINT AND WORK ON YOUR TEMPERAMENT

Group: Take a hint and work on your temperament.
Student 1:   When I am cheerful and full of joy, I can get along with other girls and boys.

Group: Take a hint and work on your temperament.
Student 2:   When I am feeling moody or bad, I shouldn't blame others for the day I've had.

Group: Take a hint and work on your temperament.
Student 3:   If I am ever nasty or mean, I need to hide and not be seen.

Group: Take a hint and work on your temperament.
Student 4:   When my temper gets hot, my friends and family won't like me a lot.

Group: Take a hint and work on your temperament.
Student 5:   When I am sweet and kind, more friends I will make, keep, and find.

Group: Take a hint and work on your temperament.
Student 6:   If I am heartless or cold, people won't want to be near me I'm told.

Group: Take a hint and work on your temperament.
Student 7:   When I am feeling sad or blue, helping someone else is what I can do.

Group: Take a hint and work on your temperament.
Student 8:   If I am cynical or cruel, kids won't care to be around me at school.

Group: Take a hint and work on your temperament.
Student 9:   If I feel violent or want to lash out, getting in control is what I should be about.

Group: Take a hint and work on your temperament.
Student 10: When I am patient and polite, things will turn around and be all right.

Group: Take a hint and work on your temperament.

SHARE== CARE ==AND ==BE ==FAIR

Share, care and be fair
Work on sharing, caring, and being fair

Work on caring about your future
Work on caring about your life
Develop more self-control
To relieve some stresses and strife

Work on being tolerate
Work on being fair
And a lot of your disappointments
Will be easier to bare

Work on being friendly
When playing sports or games
Don't be a sore loser
By calling your teammates names

Share your possessions
Share your toys
Try not to be selfish
With other girls or boys

Care about your classmates
Care about your friends
Show love and affection
Without making amends

Share, care, and be fair
Share, care, and be fair
These qualities are sometimes rare
But you must be aware
That it is always good to
Share, care, and be fair

USE YOUR HEAD!

When you know something is wrong,
Without playing a different song-
                    Use your head!

When things don't feel right,
And there are no adults in sight-
                    Use your head!

If you see something bad,
And start feeling sad-
                    Use your head!

If you are away from home,
And your friends think they're grown-
                    Use your head!

When things get out of control,
And you can't hide out in a hole-
                    Use your head!

If it is past ridicule,
Follow a simple rule-
                    Use your head!

If you see someone stealing,
And it doesn't feel appealing-
                    Use your head!

If your classmates cheat on a test,
Don't focus on all the rest-
                    Use your head!

If others curse and shout,
Don't worry about standing out-
                    Use your head!

When people around you are cruel,
At least you won't be the fool-
                    Use your head!

If kids are acting mean,
You don't have to be part of that scene-
                    Use your head!

45

ACT LIKE A LADY - ACT LIKE A GENTLEMAN

Act like a lady - act like a gentleman

A lady:
> Stands tall,
> Doesn't fall,
> Talks nice,
> Seeks advice,
> Isn't loud,
> Feels proud,
> Listens well,
> Wants to excel,
> Combs her hair,
> Watches what she wears,
> Doesn't fight,
> Handles herself right,
> Is clean and neat,
> Polite and sweet,
> Is considerate and kind,
> And has school on her mind.

A gentleman:
> Stands proud,
> Isn't loud,
> Respects a lady,
> Doesn't act crazy,
> Takes the lead,
> Wants to succeed,
> Walks tall,
> Gets up after a fall,
> Helps his mother,
> Sister and brother,
> Lends a hand,
> Whenever he can,
> Doesn't fight,
> To prove he's right,
> Doesn't curse,
> Or act worse,
> Takes turns,
> Makes school his concern.

Act like a lady - act like a gentleman.

PUT GOOD BEHAVIOR 1st

If you are at home or at school,
Put good behavior 1st
And obey all the rules

> If you are going on a trip to the mall,
> Put good behavior 1st
> You can still have a ball

If you are traveling anywhere,
Put good behavior 1st
Before you get there

> If you are playing inside or out,
> Put good behavior 1st
> It's what life is all about

If you are at a grocery mart,
Put good behavior 1st
It's a better way to start

> If you are on a bus or train,
> Put good behavior 1st
> And don't act strange

If you are shopping at a store,
Put good behavior 1st
Do what is right and more

> If you are going anywhere,
> Put good behavior 1st
> So people won't stare

TEASING ISN'T PLEASING

Teasing isn't pleasing
       It's nasty and mean
Betwixt and between

It's a dirty shame
       To say ugly names
It hurts down deep
       And causes others to weep

You won't feel great
       To tease at any rate
If the tables are turned around
       The teaser wouldn't be happy, I've found

Teasing can't make you strong
       Because it is always wrong
It also causes ill will
       To annoy and mock for real

It's better to be fair
       And treat your classmates with care
If the teasing doesn't end,
       You may end up with no friends

Teasing isn't pleasing
       It's nasty and mean
Betwixt and between

CATCH YOURSELF DOING THE RIGHT THING!

Catch yourself doing the right thing!
Catch yourself doing the right thing!

The right thing is:
> To never steal
> Work for what you want
> Don't do it for the thrill

Catch yourself doing the right thing!
Catch yourself doing the right thing!

The right thing is:
> To never cheat
> Study for your tests
> Stand on your own two feet

Catch yourself doing the right thing!
Catch yourself doing the right thing!

The right thing is:
> To stop the fighting
> Hurting others is wrong
> Settle things peacefully
> We all can get along

Catch yourself doing the right thing!
Catch yourself doing the right thing!

The right thing is:
> To stop the cursing
> Bad words hurt
> Don't treat others
> Like rubbish or dirt

Catch yourself doing the right thing!
Catch yourself doing the right thing!

IT'S WORTH THE TIME; IT'S WORTH THE EFFORT

It's worth the time; it's worth the effort
A kind word is always clearly heard

It's worth the time; it's worth the effort
A thoughtful deed helps others in need

It's worth the time; it's worth the effort
Teaching the world to love is what we need more of

It's worth the time; it's worth the effort
A smile a day goes a long, long way

It's worth the time; it's worth the effort
Building trust is an absolute must

It's worth the time; it's worth the effort
A pleasant greeting will cheer the ones you are meeting

It's worth the time; it's worth the effort
Thoughtfulness and sharing is a nice form of caring

It's worth the time; it's worth the effort
Taking turns is a good way to learn

It's worth the time; it's worth the effort
Waiting patiently in line is the best way I find

It's worth the time; it's worth the effort
Listen and hear with an understanding ear

It's worth the time; it's worth the effort
Settle arguments and fights by doing something right

It's worth the time; it's worth the effort
A friend is a treasure beyond any measure

It's worth the time; it's worth the effort
Keep calm and in control so you can reach a particular goal
It's worth the time; it's worth the effort

CHECK THE TIME — CHECK YOURSELF

Check the Time - Check Yourself
In the morning, at night
Check to see if you're acting right!

>Check the Time - Check Yourself
>At school, at home
>Even when you're all alone!

Check the Time - Check Yourself
With your family, with your friends
Check yourself over and over again!

>Check the Time - Check Yourself
>At work, at play
>Each and everyday!

Check the Time - Check Yourself
At a library, or at a park
During the day or when its dark!

>Check the Time - Check Yourself
>At a mall, or at a store
>Check yourself, not less, but more!

Check the Time - Check Yourself
Don't scream, push, or fight
Check to see if you're acting right!

>Check the Time - Check Yourself
>Learn to be calm and polite
>Check to see if you're acting right!

Chapter III.

Values
Are Vital

The verses presented in Chapter III demonstrate how poetry can be used as a method to reduce violent or disruptive behavior. This chapter also focuses on key qualities that make people unique. Several selections direct children to always express their feelings in a socially acceptable manner.

* Numerous Character Development Programs are analogous to some Values Education Programs and can incorporate many of the materials presented in this section. The poems or theme centered pieces can always be adapted or changed to fit the situation or persons involved.

* For instance, 'I Value You - You Value Me' is a poem which can be used to emphasize the importance of accepting individuals as they are without criticism or fault.

* 'Respect Others- Respect Yourself ' and 'Respect is Recognizing Someone's Worth' can be utilized in role playing with accompanying props or pictures showing how to respect other people.

* Furthermore, the poems, 'Everybody Counts-Everybody Matters', along with ' Let's Celebrate The Differences' highlight the beauty of diversity.

* 'A Student's Code of Ethics' is a good example of displaying a code of conduct for students to follow.

* It can be noted that the poem, ' All People Are Beautiful' is a perfect model for stressing the value of human life.

Overall, Chapter III serves as a vehicle to translate the message that, "We all have value so we need to value our differences".

TEN KEY QUALITIES

There are ten key qualities that work effectively
To make a better person for all to see
Ten key qualities can easily be
A guide for you and a guide for me

1. Trustworthiness -   means that others can count on you to do what you say
                        and promise, too.

2. Responsibility -   means that in being dependable and reliable as well,
                        leaves plenty of room for us all to excel.

3. Citizenship -   means that by abiding by the rules, you can be a better
                        person at home and at school.

4. Compassion -   means that by showing kindness, sympathy,
                        and heart, a better way to form friendships
                        can start.

5. Integrity -   means that by holding on to principles that are high,
                        you can do better than just getting by.

6. Respect -   means to show high regard or consideration for,
                        persons you meet now or before.

7. Fairness -   means that in sharing and taking turns, you can
                        cooperate and most of all learn.

8. Honesty -   means that in being truthful and sincere, strong values
                        can be held equally dear.

9. Discipline -   means that self-control can be an attainable goal.

10. Perseverance -   means that in working hard and not giving in, you can
                        move forward to achieve and win.

These ten key qualities work together well
To help anyone achieve and excel
What a big difference these key qualities make
In building character that is first rate!

RESPECT OTHERS - RESPECT YOURSELF

Group: Respect others, respect yourself.

Girls: Respect your teachers, family and friends.
Help others in need and have good messages to send.

Group: Respect others, respect yourself.

Boys: Everyone is different. We all have certain ways.
Diversity is good. Listen to what we have to say.

Group: Respect others, respect yourself.

Girls: Respect other's opinions, respect their feelings, too.
If someone doesn't agree, there is something you can do.

Group: Respect others, respect yourself.

Boys: Listen to your parents, listen to what they have to say.
Treat your classmates kindly because you may need them one day.

Group: Respect others, respect yourself.

Girls: Be concerned about your neighbors at any time or place.
Remember we are all part of the human race.

Group: Respect others, respect yourself.

Boys: Everyone has problems.
We all have special needs.
To bring this into focus, the advice we should heed-

Group: Respect others, respect yourself.

COMPASSION SHOULD BE IN ACTION

Compassion should be in action
At work, at play, each and everyday

Compassion should be in action
It is the consideration of the heart
From which good feelings can start
It is feeling someone's pain
So they won't suffer in vain

It is sympathy and tenderness
From an understanding quest
It is the charity of concern
From which we all can learn
It is comforting and supportive, too
A humane thing to do
It is a benevolent word
That can be internally heard
It is a feeling like no other
To share with one another

Compassion comes in many forms
To go beyond what is norm

When we show compassion, we show we care
When we show compassion, it's a way to share

We all have problems
We all have pains
When we show compassion
Everyone gains

I VALUE YOU- YOU VALUE ME

I value you
You value me
That's the way
It's supposed to be

I value you
You value me
That's the way
It's supposed to be

I value your thoughts
I value what you say
It's important to share
Each and everyday

I value your goals
I value your dreams
I value you as a person
Together, we make a team

I value your race
I value your customs, too
It's good to know
These special things about you

I value you
You value me
That's the way
It's supposed to be

I value you
You value me
It is good to connect
So readily

All people are beautiful -
    Big people
    Little people
    Fat people
    Skinny people

All people are beautiful -
    Blondes
    Brunettes
    Redheads
    Those with white hair, too

All people are beautiful -
    Dark people
    Light people
    Brown people
    White people

All people are beautiful -
    Tall people
    Short people
    Wide people
    Slim people

All people are beautiful -
    Old people
    Young people
    Physically challenged and
    Blind people

People come in many sizes and shapes, too
The world is full of people like me and like you
Different people live here and there
Yet, we are all on this earth to love and share

LET'S CELEBRATE THE DIFFERENCES

Let's celebrate the differences
At any rate, let's celebrate
Today in a positive way

Let's celebrate the differences in our names
Wouldn't it be boring if we all had the same?

Let's celebrate the differences of our faces
How wonderful it is to have so many races!

Let's celebrate the differences in our clothes
Look at the patterns of these things and those!

Let's celebrate the differences of our hair
Notice the textures and styles people wear

Let's celebrate the differences in our color and skin tones
What a strange world it would be if all people were cloned?

Let's celebrate the differences in our thoughts
In sharing, we can teach and be taught

Let's celebrate the differences in our foods
There are a variety of tastes to fit a variety of moods

Let's celebrate the colors of our eyes
Some are blue, brown, sad or wise

Let's celebrate the shades of our skin
Think of the tones again and again

Let's celebrate the differences
At any rate, let's celebrate
Let's celebrate the differences
Isn't it great to celebrate?

EVERYBODY COUNTS - EVERYBODY MATTERS

Everybody counts- everybody matters
If you are big or tall
Short, disabled or small

Everybody counts- everybody matters

If you are thin or fat,
Let me reiterate that

Everybody counts- everybody matters

If your hair is red or brown
Either way I have found

Everybody counts- everybody matters

If your race is white or black
Or if your name is Mary or Jack

Everybody counts- everybody matters

If your voice is high or low
If a person is friend or foe

Everybody counts- everybody matters

If your beard is short or long
All people on the earth belong

Everybody counts- everybody matters

If your eyes are brown or green
There is no difference in between

Everybody counts- everybody matters

If you can count to ten
Practice this over again

Everybody counts- everybody matters

A STUDENT'S CODE OF ETHICS

A student's code of ethics
Can open many doors
It is a basic list
For students to follow and more

A student's code of ethics
Can be practiced readily
On a regular basis
So easily

As a student:
I will be responsible for my actions.
I will improve my attitude and behavior.
I will open my mind to learning and knowledge.
I will demonstrate good sportsmanship.
I will organize my materials and supplies.
I will be sensitive to the opinions, feelings, and beliefs of others.
I will solve problems peacefully.
I will seek help and assistance with my homework and matters that concern me.
I will calm my temper and emotions when I am upset or angry.
I will think before I react.
I will abide by the rules.
I will respect my fellow classmates and teachers at all times
I will make myself available when someone needs my help or assistance.
I will share my time and talents.
I will be a good example to younger students and siblings.
I will discipline myself to resist peer pressure.
I will not respond negatively to correction or discipline.
I will stay cool, calm, and in control.
I will not resort to violence to solve disputes or disagreements.
I will use good grammar and speech.
I will not seek revenge for hurt feelings or disappointments.
I will help my parents at home and my teachers at school.
I will practice reading on a daily basis.
I will give unselfishly.
I will remember that my actions may cause a reaction in others.
I will recognize the fact that life is a journey to be traveled carefully and well.

IT'S ALWAYS GOOD TO TELL THE TRUTH

It's always good to tell the truth

If you lie one time
It takes another one to fix it
If you lie two times
You need two plus two more
To even the score

If you lie three times
It takes three plus three
To try to get free

If you lie four times
It takes four times four more
Before things hit the floor

If you lie five times
Five plus five times five
Adds up to a lot of jive

If you lie six times
Six times six times six
Means you'll be counting with more than sticks

If you lie seven times
Seven by seven by seven
Won't get you into heaven

If you lie eight times
Eight times eight by eighty-eight
Means you are going down at a very fast rate

If you lie nine times
Ninety-nine times ninety-nine
You are running out of reasons and rhymes

If you lie ten times
Ten multiplied by ten hundred and ten
Starts the cycle all over again!

It's always good to tell the truth
It's always good to tell the truth

DON'T HATE WHEN YOU CAN APPRECIATE

Don't hate when you can appreciate
Don't hate when you can appreciate

Appreciate your home
You could be out there alone

Appreciate your kin
Respect them again and again

Appreciate your neighbors
You might have to ask them for a favor

Appreciate your race
And the distinctive features of your face

Appreciate your food
And the variety of tastes to fit the mood

Appreciate your clothes
And the ability to choose from these or those

Appreciate your life
And all that it brings

Appreciate yourself
Before anything

DON'T HOLD A GRUDGE

Don't hold a grudge
Or bite a nail of hate
And fail to appreciate

Don't hold a grudge
And keep things in
And force yourself to grin

Don't hold a grudge
Because that tight, hard knot
May fester in a pot

Don't hold a grudge
Because your temper may explode
And spill a nasty load

Don't hold a grudge
And clinch your teeth
And harden underneath

Don't hold a grudge
And fail to forgive
It may affect the way you live

Don't hold a grudge
And turn cold
With disagreements that are old

RESPECT IS RECOGNIZING SOMEONE'S WORTH

Group: Respect is recognizing someone's worth.
Everyone is important on this earth.
Respect is recognizing someone's worth.
Everyone is important on this earth.

Student 1: I respect your opinions. I respect your views. I respect your decisions; it's good to hear something new.

Group: Respect is recognizing someone's worth.
Everyone is important on this earth.
Respect is recognizing someone's worth.
Everyone is important on this earth.

Student 2: I respect your feelings. I respect your needs; I respect your ideas, let's help each other succeed.

Group: Respect is recognizing someone's worth.
Everyone is important on this earth.
Respect is recognizing someone's worth.
Everyone is important on this earth.

Student 3: I respect your language and your customs, too. There are so many things I can learn about you.
Group: Respect is recognizing someone's worth.
Everyone is important on this earth.
Respect is recognizing someone's worth.
Everyone is important on this earth.

Student 4: I respect your habits. I respect your plans; I respect your wishes across this magnificent land.
Group: Respect is recognizing someone's worth.
Everyone is important on this earth.
Respect is recognizing someone's worth.
Everyone is important on this earth.

Student 5: I respect how you think. I respect what you say; we are all unique in a very special way.
Group: Respect is recognizing someone's worth.
Everyone is important on this earth.
Respect is recognizing someone's worth.
Everyone is important on this earth.

Student 6:   I respect your family. I respect your friends. I respect your home; there are so many ways to blend.

Group: Respect is recognizing someone's worth.
              Everyone is important on this earth.
              Respect is recognizing someone's worth.
              Everyone is important on this earth.

Student 7:   I respect your color; I respect your race. I respect your heritage and the beauty of your face.

Group: Respect is recognizing someone's worth.
              Everyone is important on this earth.
              Respect is recognizing someone's worth.
              Everyone is important on this earth.

Student 8:   I respect your community and the people on your block. I respect all of the things that we can share and unlock.

Group: Respect is recognizing someone's worth.
              Everyone is important on this earth.
              Respect is recognizing someone's worth.
              Everyone is important on this earth.

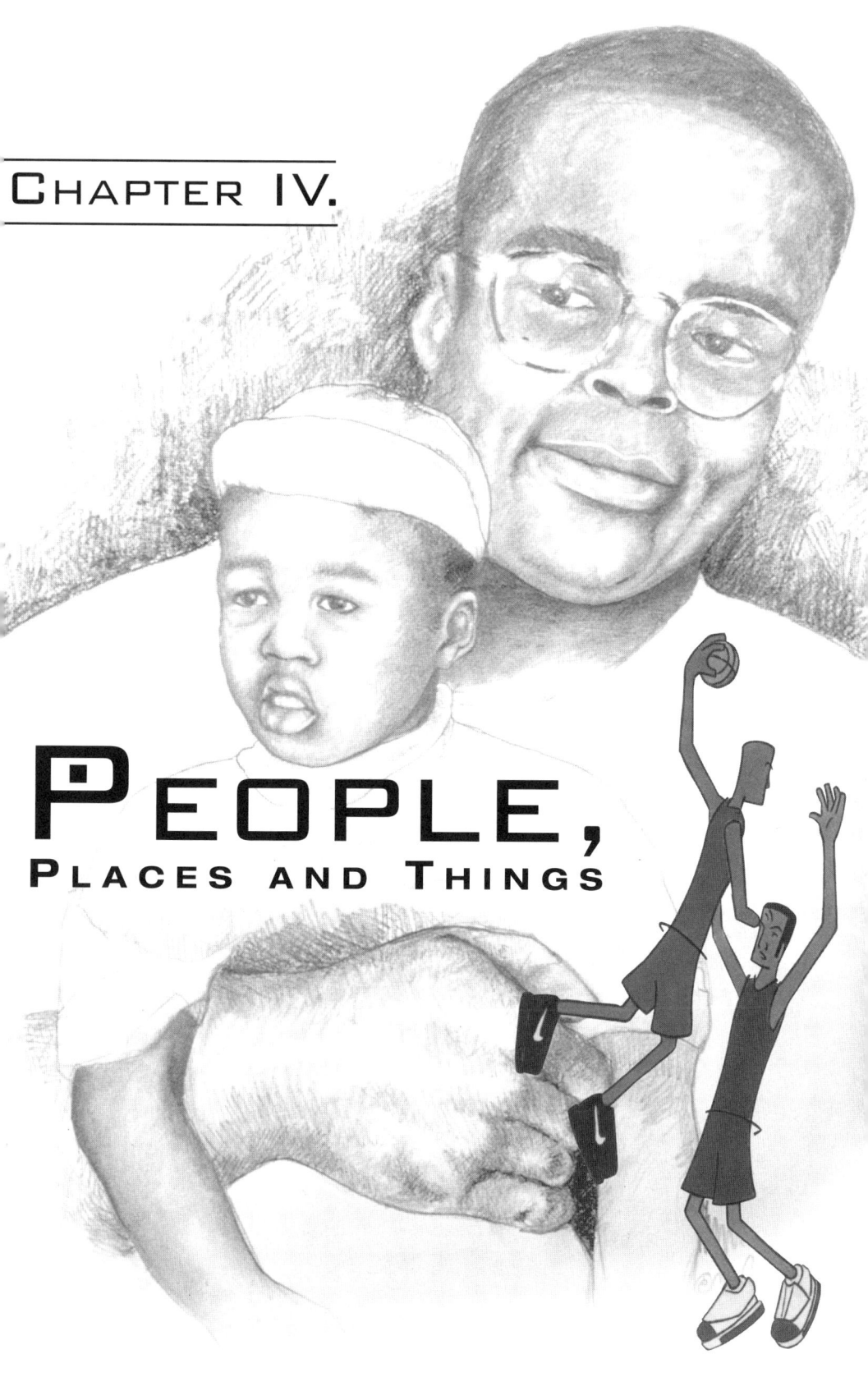

CHAPTER IV.

PEOPLE,
PLACES AND THINGS

Chapter IV recognizes the fact that people,

places, and things affect children in various

ways.

* Parents are central figures in influencing the thoughts, feelings, and attitudes of youngsters. They are in a critical position to instruct their child on a daily basis.

* Teachers have an opportunity to mold the minds and hearts of children as well. They can also help calm and clarify issues that concern their students directly. For example, a teacher may take a newsworthy item of a school shooting or an act of violence to teach moral lessons through poetry.

* One way to do this is to have the children write an acrostic or alphabet poem. An example of this would be to have the children write the letters of a given word horizontally down a sheet of paper. The students would then be directed to write a word for each particular letter.

* If the word is 'Hate', the students can write a positive word to represent each letter in 'Hate'. A word for the letter' h' could be 'harmony',

and an 'a' word ' attitude.' The 't' word could be 'tolerance' and an 'e' word could be 'equality'. This process could generate wonderful pieces that would promote thought and creativity.

* Likewise, the poems in this chapter could also be used to show how different people and things have power and influence.

* Examples of poems using people in a positive light would be 'Work Together as a Family', 'Parents/Teachers Invest in Your Student's Success' and 'Fathers Are Needed'.

* The poems, 'Change Can Be Beautiful', and 'It Takes Teamwork' denote important concepts that can help develop a child's character.

PARENTS MAKE A WORLD OF DIFFERENCE

Parents make a world of difference.
A big, wide world of difference, parents make.
A world that can be seen, felt, and heard.
Parents make a world of difference in the lives of their children.
They make a difference in:

> A-Attitudes
> B-Beliefs
> C -Confidence
> D-Decision Making
> E -Examples
> F -Feelings
> G -Guidance
> H -Habits
> I - Improvement
> J - Judgment
> K-Knowledge
> L -Learning
> M-Morals
> N-Nurturing
> O-Opinions
> P-Performance
> Q-Qualifications
> R-Responsibility
> S-Stability
> T-Tolerance
> U-Unity
> V-Values
> W-Work Ethic
> X-Extra Curricular Activities
> Y-Yesterday, Today, and Tomorrow
> Z- Zeal for life and living

Parents make a world of difference.
A big, wide world of difference, parents make.

Parents make a world of difference.
A big difference in the world!

SOMEONE IS WAITING

Someone is waiting at your door
To help you with problems, give answers and more

Someone is waiting with love at the end
It could be a neighbor, your parent, or friend

Someone is waiting with outstretched arms
To give you comfort and to keep you from harm

Someone is waiting with a tender touch
To give you the support that means so much

Someone is waiting with each passing day
To guide and direct and show you the way

Someone is waiting to take your hand
And lead you forward across this land

Someone is waiting in the shadows or light
To give you assistance both day and night

THE CRITICAL THINKING ALPHABET

The Critical Thinking Alphabet
Is listed for you to see
How important the Thinking Skills are
Alphabetically

There are 26 letters
To think about and learn
They stress major features
Of interest and concern

There is no secret recipe. Just remember the following A B C's:

A - association
B - brainstorming
C - classification
D - definition
E - evaluation
F - factual
G - generalization
H - hypothesizing
I - inference
J - judging
K -knowledge
L - logic
M -modification
N -noteworthy
O - organization
P - prioritizing
Q- questioning
R - reasoning
S- sequencing
T -thought
U - utilize
V - visualization
W - weigh
X -examine
Y - yield
Z - zeroing into all of the

Critical Thinking letters
So you can think and reason better!

BLACK FAMILY

Black family
Live together
Give together

        Stay together
        Pray together

Work together
Play together
        Eat together
        Be together

Give more to each other
Right where you are

Don't break-up, Make -up
Don't Fight, Forgive

Greet each other - Meet each other
-------------- Halfway -----------------

Vow to make each other proud
Grow in Understanding and Awareness

Form a bond of Mutual Respect and Admiration
Be Adaptable and Available and Accountable

Live -------- Laugh -------- and ---------- Love

Choose to be happy in each other's world

And, when trials or tribulations occur
Stand on solid ground and hold fast
With linking hearts and hands

You will become a Family United
Face the world as one!

THE WAY TO REALLY FLY IS BY

The way to really fly and score high is by:

> Reading everyday,
> Solving math problems,
> Counting money,
> Staying in school,
> Controlling your emotions,
> Doing your homework,
> Stopping bad habits,
> Being on time,
> Being courteous,
> Showing kindness,
> Having pride in yourself,
> Taking time to listen,
> Helping others,
> Staying in control,
> Caring about others,
> Respecting adults,
>   And,
> Being Responsible.

You can run like a train if you refrain from:

> Cursing,
> Fighting,
> Lying,
> Cheating,
> Stealing,
> Hitting,
> Teasing,
>   And,
> Intimidating.

The way to really fly is by making an effort to try
Then, you can run like a train and from violence, refrain!

PARENTS: YOU HAVE THE POWER AND INFLUENCE

Parents, you have the power and influence.
Small faces turn to you each day for guidance. Think about your life and the way you are living.

Parents, you have the power and influence.
Bright, eager eyes look to you for love and affection. Open your hands and hearts to show that you care.

Parents, you have the power and influence.
Tiny feet need someone to follow. Walk and talk with purpose and conviction.

Parents, you have the power and influence.
Short arms reach out for your help and reassurance. Extend your hand in friendship and support.

Parents, you have the power and influence.
Little minds test your strength and endurance. Carry yourself with dignity and control during times of change or challenge.

Parents, you have the power and influence.
Two big eyes see and two big ears hear everything. Watch what you say and, especially do.

Parents, you have the power and influence.
Little stomachs are always hungry. Nourish their bodies with good wholesome meals and nourish their minds with praise and encouragement.

Parents, you have the power and influence.
Parents, you have the influence and power.

Children are not little adults. They are young, small people that grow mentally, physically, emotionally, and spiritually with time and patience. Children can be taught to be kind, compassionate, and unselfish human beings. They can succeed and achieve in this world with your help and guidance.

Parents, you have the power and influence.
Parents, you have the influence and power.

I AM YOUR REPORT CARD

I am your report card.
I hold all of your grades.

If you do nice work, I won't be ashamed or afraid.
Teachers, put good grades on me for my parents to see.

Student 1: If I have an "A ", I'll be happy today!

Student 2: If I have a "B", I will beam beautifully.

Student 3: If there is a "C", I must be careful and more concerned, to do a better job to study and learn.

Student 4: Look out for "D's!" I definitely need to do more to improve my grades and scores.

Student 5: A "F" it is true shows that I have failed through and through. I better beware and study with care.

Your conduct and your attitude are a part of you.
They are equally important on your report card, too.

Watch out for checks!
They point to certain behaviors or rules that need special attention at home or at school.

We all can't make "A's" and "B's" in everything we do.
But, make sure that your report card is a good reflection of you!

GET ON THE TRAIN OF ACHIEVEMENT AND GAIN

Get on the train of achievement and gain
Get on the train of achievement and gain

Gain Knowledge
From reading and math
Do all you can
To stay on the right path

Gain Confidence
And, improve your self-esteem
Treat others with respect
Don't be hostile or mean

Gain Control
Of your emotions and more
Having a cool, calm demeanor
Will open many doors

Gain Peace and Love
In your heart
Accept people as they are
Right from the start

Gain Self-esteem
Gain the power within
Be patient and kind
Be flexible and bend

Gain Wisdom
Learn all that you can
Strive to do better
From where you stand

Gain Experiences
From life and living
And remember to be tolerate
And especially forgiving

Get on the train of achievement and gain
Get on the train of achievement and gain

YOU'VE GOT A REAL FRIEND

You've got a real friend
When he's there in need,
And wants you to succeed

You've got a real friend
When he listens well,
And your secrets won't tell

You've got a real friend
When he shares your concerns,
And wants to take turns

You've got a real friend
If he shows he cares,
When others aren't there

You've got a real friend
When he is near or around,
When you are feeling down

You've got a real friend
If you're feeling sad or blue,
Your friend will be there for you

THE HOOD IS YOUR NEIGHBORHOOD

The hood is your neighborhood
The hood is your neighborhood

What can you do to keep it nice?
You can:

Rake the leaves and practice saying, " please"

Help your neighbors by doing them a favor

Don't talk loud and make your parents proud

Cut the grass and bag the yard waste fast

Turn the radio down; it's better all around

Pick up dirt and trash and recycle cans for cash

Watch out for strangers; they could mean danger

Clean up your yard or play a friendly game of cards

Obey traffic lights and keep valuables out of sight

Call the police so that crimes won't increase

Be careful crossing the street and be courteous to those you meet

Keep the sidewalks clear and pick up cans of beer

Take pride in what you do and welcome people that are new

The hood is your neighborhood
The hood is your neighborhood

Keep things nice at any price.

PARENTS: IMPROVE YOUR HOME AND FAMILY ENVIRONMENT

Parents, improve your home and family environment
Use the following a b c's correctly:

> A - Allow time for study
> B - Be available for help
> C - Care about what your child is learning
> D - Don't change your rules or regulations
> E - Eagerly meet your child everyday
> F - Find time to reflect on the days events
> G - Go to Report Card Pick-ups
> H - Have Family Forums to solve problems
> I - Involve your child in activities
> J - Join forces with your child's teacher
> K - Keep positive and productive
> L - Learn to listen
> M - Make promises that you will keep
> N - Never give up
> 0 - Organize schedules to have dinner together
> P - Plan family outings
> Q - Quiet the house during homework time
> R - Respect your child's feelings and opinions
> S - Shower your kids with love not gifts
> T - Take your child to church, don't send him
> U - Understand that children are not miniature adults
> V - Vow to be a better parent
> W - Work with your child everyday
> X - Examine your attitude frequently and adjust it
> Z - Zero into changes in your child's behavior

Parents, improve your home and family environment
By practicing these a b c's -
Then your child's behavior
Can change dramatically

CULTIVATE A FRIENDSHIP

Cultivate a friendship
Like a flower in a bed
Nourish it and tend to it
And pull the doubts of dread

> Cultivate a friendship
> With rays from the sun
> And cool refreshing waters
> As soon as the work is done

Cultivate a friendship
Patient hands will tend
To wants and wishes
Around the garden bend

> Cultivate a friendship
> With tender loving care
> So as not to disturb
> The closeness there

Cultivate a friendship
And when weeds do appear
Pull them by the roots
Until the ground is clear

> Cultivate a friendship
> With love and good cheer
> So that all of the plants
> Will sprout anew each year

Cultivate a friendship
With sweet drops of rain
So in times of drought
Life won't be in vain

> Cultivate a friendship
> And allow each precious flower
> To be anchored in love
> And grow stronger by the hour

GET ON THE BALL AND BE PRACTICAL!

Get on the ball and be practical!
Get on the ball and be practical!

Get extra rest before a test!

Stand tall and start over if you fall!

Watch what you think and say everyday!

Study well so you won't fail!

Save your cash so that it will last!

Be ready to learn and for your future be concerned!

Check the weather at night so the next day you can dress right!

Don't lose your cool and stay in school!

Always do more to improve your grades and scores!

Turn your work in on time without giving excuses or rhymes!

Don't get uptight when things don't turn out right!

Have your homework ready and don't focus on things that are petty!

Stay away from drugs and especially thugs!

Get on the ball and be practical!
Get on the ball and be practical!

DON'T LOCK OUT YOUR PARENTS

Don't lock out your parents
Don't lock them out
They have knowledge and wisdom
They know what life is about

Don't lock out your parents
And throw away the key
Keeping them in the dark
Away from your world to see

Don't lock out your parents
By not talking to them
They have had many experiences
Don't rely on your emotions or whims

Don't lock out your parents
By ignoring them sometimes
They want to help you
And keep you in line

Don't lock out your parents
They are a part of you
Share in each other's world
And you will make it through

CHANGE CAN BE BEAUTIFUL!

Change can be beautiful!
It will allow you to grow
And move with the flow

    Change can be beautiful!
    It will give you a view
    That is totally brand new

Change can be beautiful!
It will allow you to look
At a different kind of book

    Change can be beautiful!
    It will allow you to change
    And your affairs rearrange

    Change can be beautiful!
    It will allow you to rest
    And reaffirm your quest

    Change can be beautiful!
    It will answer the call
    For you to get on the ball

    Change can be beautiful!
    It will help you explore
    The horizon and more

    Change can be beautiful!
    It can be beautiful -
    When you are willing to
    change!

IT TAKES TEAMWORK

What does it take?
It takes teamwork, teamwork.
What makes work great?
It takes teamwork, teamwork.

TEAMWORK is the unit
That comes together
When forces are joined,
In all types of weather

The letters in TEAMWORK
Are spelled out for you
To explore all of the skills
And the jobs you must do

T - is for Time
       Time must be spent
       To get the work done
       From the smallest task
       To the largest one

E - is for Effort
       There must be a joint effort
       From all the people and more
       Working hard together
       So production will soar

A - is for Attendance
       Attendance is vital
       So is being on time
       A group can work better
       Without excuses or rhymes

M - is for Management
       Management must be present
       To handle and control
       Job distribution
       To achieve a goal

W - is for Work
>Work is the labor
>To get the task done
>From the difficult deeds
>To the easy ones

0 - is for Order
>Things must be in order
>From the beginning to the end
>Everyone must be flexible
>And especially blend

R - is for Responsibility
>Responsibility is important
>To work with any team
>To meet obligations
>No matter how hard things seem

K - is for Knowledge
>Knowledge to understand
>What teamwork is about
>It is gained experience
>Which leaves little room for doubt

What does it take?
It takes teamwork, teamwork.
What makes work great?
It takes teamwork, teamwork.

WORK TOGETHER AS A FAMILY

Work together as a family
When there are chores to be done -
Try to include everyone

Work together as a family
When there are leaves to be raked -
Working together makes the task great

Work together as a family
When there is shopping to do -
Dividing up the list is easier, too

Work together as a family
To get the kitchen clean -
Work together as a team

Work together as a family
When the furniture needs to be dusted -
More hands can be trusted

Work together as a family
When life gets crazy -
Together, no one gets lazy

Work together as a family
When the garbage needs to go out -
Take turns so nobody shouts

Work together as a family
When there is any job to do -
Everyone working together can see things through

PARENTS/ TEACHERS: INVEST IN YOUR STUDENT'S SUCCESS

Parents/Teachers invest in your students' success. Consider the terms used in banking to help your students succeed in life.

1. Make daily Deposits of Love and Affection.
2. Invest in Time and Togetherness.
3. Protect Interests and Secrets.
4. Spend a Percentage of each day Reading.
5. Give Credit for Good Behavior.
6. Establish a Savings Plan for Trips and Fun Activities.
7. Share Treasured Items and Memories.
8. Withdraw Negative Feelings and Attitudes.
9. Forgive and Forget Past Accounts.
10. Record Grades and Achievements.
11. Regulate Anger and Hate.
12. Find Common Interests and Skills.
13. Debit Bad Behavior and Habits.
14. Form a Cash Station of Cooperation.
15. Profit from each other's Experiences.
16. Transfer Positive Messages.
17. Authorize Regular Statements of Love.
18. Issue Praise not Criticism.
19. Loan Trust.
20. Cash in on Quality Time.
21. Reserve Quiet Periods.
22. Collect Self-control.
23. Trade Places and Passions.
24. Check Homework Assignments.
25. Locate hidden Talents and Abilities.
26. Draft a Plan for Conflict Resolution.
27. Supply Unlimited Affection.
28. Note Changes in Behavior.
29. Finance Projects Together.
30. Install Learning Centers.
31. Lend a Helping Hand.
32. Allow Room to Expand.
33. Replenish Low Self-esteem.
34. Maintain a Friendly Environment.
35. Form a Bond of Mutual Love and Respect.

PLEASANT PEOPLE

Pleasant People
Are good to have around
They're more positive and productive
They smile rather than frown

Pleasant People
Keep their emotions in check
They realize that a good attitude
Gives them more respect

Pleasant People
Are more agreeable and nice
They show genuine interest
In someone's views or advice

Pleasant People
Seem to get along better
With different personalities
In all types of weather

Pleasant People
Have a good perspective, too
They also get down to business
When there is work to do

Pleasant People
Make a strong statement each day
That it is better to be pleasant
Than any other way!

IT'S NEVER TOO LATE TO UNITE A FAMILY

It's never too late to unite a family;
It's never ever too late.

It's never too late to BEGIN.
It's never too late to BELIEVE.
It's never too late to BOND.

It's never too late to unite a family;
It's never ever too late.

It's never too late to LEARN.
It's never too late to LIVE.
It's never too late to LOVE.

It's never too late to STOP.
It's never too late to LOOK.
It's never too late to LISTEN.

It's never too late to FEEL.
It's never too late to FOCUS.
It's never too late to FORGIVE.

It's never too late to ENJOY.
It's never too late to ENTERTAIN.
It's never too late to EMBRACE.

It's never too late to RESOLVE.
It's never too late to REDIRECT.
It's never too late to RENEW.

It's never too late to unite a family;
It's never, ever too late.

A SMILE IS ALWAYS WORTHWHILE

A smile is always worthwhile
It is good in the morning; it is good at night
A warm, friendly smile
Makes a cloudy day bright

A smile helps people
Glow throughout the day
It spreads a bit of sunshine
Along the way

A smile lifts your mood
To make you feel better
From sad to happy
In all types of weather

A smile can turn
A frown around
And, cool hot tempers
Down, down, down

A smile is a token
You can freely give
To anyone, anywhere
As long as you live

A smile is a gift
That you can share
It doesn't cost a penny
To have a smile to wear

OUR FLAG

Our Flag is RED, BLACK, and GREEN
RED, BLACK, and GREEN
What dignity these colors bring
RED, BLACK, and GREEN
What beautiful colors
What do they mean?
RED, BLACK, and GREEN

RED - is for the blood, struggle, or fight
Many people had to suffer
To make this country right

BLACK - is for African - Americans
A people strong and free
Living to express pride and dignity

GREEN - stands for the land and the future to be
Full of hope and opportunities

RED, BLACK, and GREEN
They are the best colors I have ever seen
RED, BLACK, and GREEN
What dignity these colors bring
RED, BLACK, and GREEN
A symbol of pride these colors mean

JUST SAYING, "THANKS"

Just saying, "thanks"
With vigor and zest
Brings happiness abound
To most earthly quests

Just saying, "thanks"
Will bring joy and ease
To life and living
If you please

Just saying, "thanks"
Will bring much more
To friends and families
From shore to shore

Just saying, "thanks"
With gratitude-
Brings flowers of love
To warm the mood

Just saying, "thanks"
Can brighten the day
And touch many hearts
Along the way

THE A B C'S OF A GOOD TEACHER

The a b c's of a good teacher
Are easy to see
That a word stands for each letter
Alphabetically
The a b c's are written
With certain qualities in mind
To make a good teacher
Of the very best kind

A good teacher:

A - Allows for individual differences.
B - Balances home, work, and school.
C - Cares about her students and parents.
D - Displays a sense of humor.
E - Expresses love and appreciation.
F - Forgives and forgets misbehavior.
G - Gives praise and positive strokes.
H - Helps without hurting self-esteem.
I - Ignores small infractions.
J - Journeys into familiar and new areas of learning.
K - Keeps control and order.
L - Learns along with her students.
M - Makes an effort to change.
N - Notices subtle changes in behavior.
0 - Omits negative words and expressions.
P - Praises small steps in the right direction.
Q - Quiets, calms, and comforts.
R - Redirects anger to promote peace.
S – Settles arguments amicably.
T - Treats everyone equally and fairly.
U - Understands the needs and interests of her students.
V - Vows to make each day positive and productive.
W - Wears a sunny smile and disposition.
X - Explains without harshness.
Y -Yields the best work from each student.
Z - Zeros into the mind, heart, and spirit of each child.

The a b c's of a good teacher
Follow a simple rule
They help guide and direct
Teachers in our schools

MOOD METER

Rate your mood
Each and everyday
Using the ten-point scale
To pave the way

If you feel good
Or, if you feel sad
Rate your mood
To reflect the day you have had

If your day goes well
Chart the number high
In rating your mood
The numbers tell how or why

If your day was bad
Things sometimes go wrong
Mark down a low number
Where it belongs

Then add up the scores
All the numbers for the week
Then think positive thoughts
And, find the answers you seek

1—2—3—4—5—6—7—8—9----10

100

PARENTS: TOUCH YOUR CHILD'S TOMORROW

Parents, touch you child's tomorrow
Take care of your child or children, today

Hug them
Help them
Hold them
Mold them

    Touch your child's tomorrow
    With hope and trust, today

Heal Hurts
Soothe Fears
Comfort Loss
Buffer Faults and Failures
Encourage Interests and Hobbies

    Touch your child's tomorrow
    With Consistency and Dedication

Discipline Fairly
Treat Equally
Make Family First
Offer Support
Take Time to Teach and Learn
Watch and Wait Patiently
Make Your Home the Base
Say Grace at Mealtimes
Allow Time for Growth and Discovery
Temper Anger and Arguments
Channel Energies in the Right Direction
Unlock Talents and Creativity
Relate to Each Other's World
Admit Mistakes
Allow Doors to Open Both Ways
Give and Take Along the Way
Foster Good Attitudes
Remember to End Each Day on a Positive Note
And, Start Each Day on a Note of Joy and Anticipation

CORNROWS, CORNROWS

Cornrows, Cornrows
Braids of hair
Carefully done
In styles to wear

Cornrows, Cornrows
Straight and neat
Rows of history
Rows complete

Cornrows, Cornrows
Can it be true?
That braids of hair
Can be woven through and through

Cornrows, Cornrows
Lines of rows
Deeply rooted
To slavery woes

Cornrows, Cornrows
Tightly bound
Holding past and future
Sound

Cornrows, Cornrows
Cultures reach
And go back far
For old to teach

Cornrows, Cornrows
Patterns go around
From mother to daughter
Homeward bound

Cornrows, Cornrows
Are hope to be
A crown of pride
For people to see

EVERYDAY IN YOUR NEIGHBORHOOD

Everyday in your neighborhood:

> **Do something right**
> **Do something good**
> **Speak up and say, "hi"**
> **To people walking by**
> **Pick up paper and trash**
> **Form friendships that will last**
> **Shake a neighbor's hand**
> **March in the school band**
> **When you are leaving wave, "good-bye"**
> **Share some apple pie**
> **Run an errand**
> **Plant flowers in a lot that is barren**
> **Deliver the newspaper**
> **Get to know the next door neighbor**
> **Help shovel the snow**
> **Offer a ride whenever you go**
> **Check on someone who is sick**
> **Pick up glass, bottles, or sticks**
> **Sweep the sidewalk**
> **Have a friendly little talk**
> **Take time to learn names**
> **Share your toys or games**
> **Read to a little kid**
> **Replace a garbage lid**
> **Wash the windows**
> **Plant flowers in a row**
> **Invite someone over to eat**
> **Collect cans on the street**
> **Rake up the leaves**
> **Trim the bushes, shrubs, or trees**
> **Cut the grass**
> **Sort paper and glass**
> **Clean the alleys, too**
> **There are so many things you can do!**

FATHERS ARE NEEDED

Father's Day comes just once a year
Yet, it is important to make perfectly clear
Fathers are needed in all walks of life
To guide their children through stresses and strife

Fathers are needed
For their strength and insight
Their wisdom and courage
Help make this world right

Fathers are needed
At home and at school
To help mold young minds
And, to enforce the rules

Fathers are needed
At work and at play
To encourage and praise
And protect along the way

Fathers are needed
Everywhere -
To nurture and sustain
And to show that they care!

DRUGS ARE NASTY BUGS

Drugs are nasty bugs
Drugs are nasty bugs

Nasty, dirty old drugs
They stink and smell
So you don't feel well

Drugs are nasty bugs
Drugs are nasty bugs

Nasty, filthy old drugs
That will rob and steal
Your life for real

Drugs are nasty bugs
Drugs are nasty bugs

Nasty, mean old drugs
That can cheat and creep
And keep you from a restful sleep

Drugs are nasty bugs
Drugs are nasty bugs

Nasty, foul old drugs
They will give you problems and pains
From all drugs, refrain

Drugs are nasty bugs
Nasty bugs are drugs

PARENTS: MOTIVATE YOUR CHILD

Parents, you can motivate your child to be a better student. There are key things that you can do, to be a better parent through and through.

1. <u>Be a Consistent Parent</u>. If you have certain rules or limits, enforce them all of the time. Realize that good rules serve a good purpose and abide by them.

2. <u>Be a Respectful Parent</u>. Let your children see you respect teachers, neighbors, store personnel, policemen, and firefighters, etc. Children see and hear how you treat others so set a good example.

3. <u>Be a Responsible Parent</u>. Have chores and deadlines for everyone in the family. Always follow through with your promises and punishments. Try to be dependable and accountable in everything you do.

4. <u>Be an Encouraging Parent</u>. Sprinkle praise with constructive criticism as needed. If your child exhibits bad behavior, let him know that you love him, but not his behavior or actions. Always urge your child to do his best. Never hold back love or praise for special times or favors.

5. <u>Be an Attentive Parent</u>. It is easier to talk and lecture than it is to listen. Take time to listen with an understanding ear.

6. <u>Be a Communicative Parent</u>. Ask open-ended questions that allow conversation to flow freely. Don't be demanding, discuss.

7. <u>Be a Loving Parent</u>. Show unconditional love, care, and concern. Your child is never too old for a hug or handshake.

8. <u>Be a Supportive Parent</u>. Get involved in what your child is doing; cheer him on in sports, praise his accomplishments and attend school functions. Cultivate your child's special interests and abilities.

9. <u>Be an Understanding Parent</u>. Realize that your child is at a different stage of development than you are. Learn to appreciate where you both are at this particular day and time.

10. <u>Be a Happy Parent</u>. When you are happy and secure, your child will have some stability. Spend time with your child and time to pursue your own interests as well.

Parents, you can motivate your child to be a better student and a better person in life.

Parents don't forget to be:
Consistent,
Respectful,
Responsible,
Encouraging,
Attentive,
Communicative,
Loving,
Supportive,
Understanding,
And
Happy in Your Pursuit of Excellence!

Parents, motivate your child.
Practice these points everyday
To make your child a better person
Must start with you today!

FATHERS ARE EVERYWHERE

Fathers are everywhere
Take Time to notice them
Take Time to appreciate them
Take Time to behold them

Fathers are everywhere
Notice their strength
Notice their stature
Notice their substance

Fathers are everywhere
On the corners, down the hall
In offices or by the wall
In doorways, upstairs
Watching television on sofas or chairs

Fathers are everywhere
Driving trucks, or driving cars
Many live close while others live far
Countless are thoughtful, while many have had
Experiences that make them proud to be a dad

Fathers are everywhere
In churches and in schools
Some have occupations that require strict rules
Some are in cities, and several by the shore
Most have the time to help their children and more

Fathers are everywhere
In the theaters, on the bus
Many know education is a must
Some are professional, neat and clean
A number are sincere and are proud to be seen

Fathers are everywhere
Most are unselfish, generous, and kind
Many are available or are easy to find
Some are lean while others are stout
A number of fathers have plenty of clout

Fathers are everywhere
Many fathers recognize their power and worth,
And realize their significance on this earth

Fathers are everywhere
Everywhere indeed
Let's encourage our fathers because
Their presence we need!

TWO CLASSMATES

Two classmates
So close and near
Stay together
Every year

    Two classmates
    Side by side
    Unspoken bonds of love
    Can't hide

        Two classmates
        Inseparable it's true
        Always come together
        In a package of two

            Two classmates
            Never one without the other
            Sharing good times
            Like sister and brother

                Two classmates
                During times of stress or strife
                Stay connected
                All throughout life

DR. MARTIN LUTHER KING

Dr. King,
January 15th is your birthday
A day to celebrate
A day to remember that you were great
You led this nation
To do what was right
To stand for Justice
And not to fight
You told us to, "Dream"
You told us to, "Pray"
You said, "We Will Overcome Someday"
We must walk hand in hand
With one another
And to treat our enemies
Like our brothers
You told us to, "Love"
You told us to, "Live"
You told us to, "Learn"
Not to "Hate" and "Forgive"
In all that we do
In all that we say -
Dr. Martin Luther King...
We honor you today!

PARENTS: TAKE A STAND FOR YOUR CHILDREN

Parents: Take a stand for your children
Take a stand for Rights
Take a stand for Responsibility
Take a stand for Respect
Take a stand for Reality

Parents, you have the most challenging and the most rewarding job in the world. You are your child's first teacher, role model, and moral guide. Parenting is very hard work.

Parents, you should be prepared to support your child emotionally, physically, spiritually, financially, and educationally.

Parents you should:

Guide and abide,
Teach and preach,
Scold and hold,
Punish and praise,
Give and receive,
Walk and talk,
Comfort and care,
Spend and bend,
Watch and wait,
Help and hug,
Read and feed,
And,
Direct and protect.

Parenthood is full of twists and turns and problems and concerns. Just remember that you have the power to overcome any challenge. Parents your job is a difficult lifetime endeavor with many pains and pleasures in between.

Parents take a stand for your child or children or they will stand with someone else.

WE ARE A COMMUNITY

We are a community
A family of one
Working together
To get the job done

We are a community
Bound by streets
With rows of houses
And yards that are neat

We are a community
Standing strong
Against the forces
That can do us wrong

We are a community
With neighbors dear
Sharing our problems
Year after year

We are a community
With determination and pride
We banish criminals
By laws we abide

We are a community
A number vast
We must be united
In purpose to last

We are a community
It proves to be true
That we will always need
Each one of you

DON'T TAKE A VACATION FROM READING

Don't take a vacation from reading!
Don't take a vacation from reading!

Summer is coming
School will be out
The days will be longer
To run all about

The nice warm weather
And the long hot days
Will make you feel lazy
In so many ways

But heed this advice
And heed it well
This time away from school
Can help you excel

READ during the day
READ during the night
Because you need the practice
To keep your scores uptight

READING is a skill
You will always need
So every summer vacation
READ! READ! READ!

Don't take a vacation from reading!
Don't take a vacation from reading!

114

DR. KING - DR. KING

Dr. King - Dr. King

> Your name is great
> What power it brings

Dr. King - Dr. King

> You were a man
> Who stood for things

Dr. King - Dr. King

> You marched for rights
> Let freedom ring

Dr. King- Dr. King

> A smart black man
> Your words have wings

Dr. King - Dr. King

> Your birthday is
> A time to sing

Dr. King - Dr. King

> With Truth and Love
> You fought for things

Dr. King - Dr. King

> We remember your words,
> "I Have A Dream"

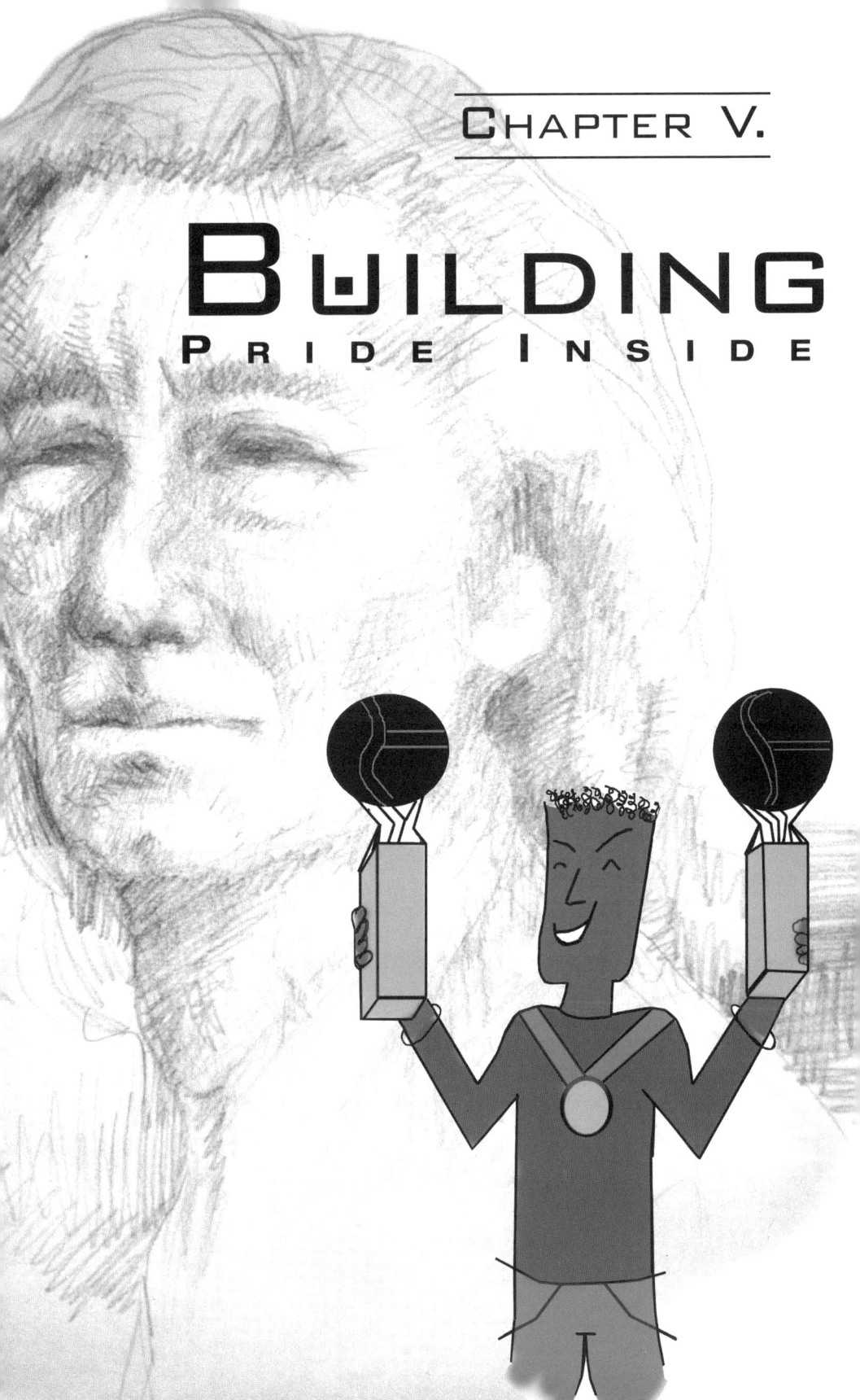

BUILDING
PRIDE INSIDE

Chapter V centers on building the qualities of self-esteem, self-confidence, and pride. The lack of these attributes may be the cause of some of the difficulties that children face at school and how they feel about themselves in general.

* Certain characteristics are essential in helping children develop into successful students and improve their self-image. Increasing a student's pride may increase his or her motivation in the process.

* Poems like 'Don't Accept Excuses' and 'Alphabet Tools For Building Self-esteem' stress significant points to direct a student on how to become more responsible and determined.

* 'Winners' is a poem with a very positive message and so is 'To Get Over, Get Better'.

* To encourage students to reach a higher level of competence, 'Make Your Goal the Honor Roll' or '20 Cans of Success' could be used. Along these lines, ' We Must Be Better Students One and All' and 'Attendance Matters' embraces the notion that

attendance and attitude are important features to recognize and improve.

Furthermore, the poems entitled, 'We've Got Pride Inside' and 'Give Me P-R-I-D-E' can be used to boost pride and self-esteem during school assembly programs or pep rallies.

PUT TO THE TEST IT'S BEST TO RELIEVE STRESS

Put to the test it's best to relieve stress
In times of trouble, or in times of need
It's good to relieve stress
To move forward and succeed

It's best to relieve stress by:
1. Focusing on the solution not the problem.
2. Choosing to be positive and optimistic.
3. Releasing negative and destructive thoughts and habits.
4. Practicing building yourself up.
5. Taking the time to heal old wounds.
6. Letting go of unnecessary people, places, and things.
7. Getting involved with a new project or activity.
8. Reading by candlelight.
9. Breaking down large tasks into smaller parts.
10. Thinking tranquil thoughts on an ocean of peace and love.
11. Turning mistakes into milestones of learning.
12. Sweeping away negative cobwebs from your mind.
13. Accepting the real situation, not an imagined one.
14. Avoiding harmful pitfalls.
15. Extending periods of rest and relaxation.
16. Changing your attitude not the attitude of others.
17. Planning ahead.
18. Writing feelings down on paper.
19. Allowing flexibility to be keynote.
20. Keeping life joyful and upbeat no matter how things look at the time.

To relieve stress in the morning
To relieve stress at night
Practice being patient, not perfect
Keep your human side in sight!

DON'T ACCEPT EXCUSES

Group: Don't accept excuses. Don't accept excuses.

Student 1:   I couldn't get my homework done because I had too many errands to run.

Student 2:   I lost my class assignment somewhere in the basement.

Group: Don't accept excuses. Don't accept excuses.

Student 3: I went somewhere with my buddy so that's the reason I couldn't study.

Student 4:   I couldn't find the right page so I went into a rage.

Group: Don't accept excuses. Don't accept excuses.

Student 5:   My dog went berserk and ate my homework.

Student 6:   I had to wait for my mother to pick up my sister and brother.

Group: Don't accept excuses. Don't accept excuses.

Student 7:   I watched television all night and the next day I couldn't think right.

Student 8:   I had nothing to wear. I couldn't do anything with my hair.

Group: Don't accept excuses. Don't accept excuses.

Student 9:   When I got home, I couldn't do my work because I was alone.

Group: Don't accept excuses. Don't accept excuses.

Student 10: I lost my pencil and pen and I didn't have time to start over again.

Group: Don't accept excuses. Don't accept excuses.

W – I – N – N – E – R – S

Winners come from many places
      They have different skills
            They have a variety of faces

Winners are people
      Who go the extra mile
            They have a good disposition and make each day worthwhile

These individuals, smile throughout the day
      They manage to always have
            Something nice to say

Winners approach life
      With vigor and zest
            They work very hard and want to do their best

They are the kind of people
      Who are friends true blue
            They are thoughtful, kind, and considerate, too

Winners don't believe
      In failure or defeat
            When winners move forward, many obstacles they beat

They keep going when
      The going gets rough
            These people are known to be tender and tough

Throughout the world
      One thought remains true–
            Winners can be people like me or like you!

ALPHABET TOOLS FOR BUILDING SELF-ESTEEM

These Alphabet Tools
Help build self-esteem
Practicing them makes sense
Now and in between

These Alphabet Tools
Show with each letter
That improved self-esteem
Can make your life better

A - Appreciate yourself at the beginning and at the end of each day.
B - Be your own best friend first.
C – Comfort yourself with praise not criticism.
D - Determine to do your best.
E - Enjoy the present and forget the past.
F - Follow directions and follow your instincts.
G -Give without expecting something in return.
H - Hug yourself for small and large victories.
I - Ignore those who want to tear you down instead of build you up.
J – Join a group or club for support.
K – Keeping upbeat and optimistic is essential.
L – Learn to listen and listen to learn.
M -Make an effort to be honest with your feelings at all times.
N - Never give up and never give in to outside pressures.
O - Organize your life, world, and affairs.
P - Prepare yourself mentally, physically, emotionally, and educationally.
Q - Quiet your mind, thoughts, and emotions.
R - Remember to stay in tune with your inner self.
S - Surround yourself with talented not toxic people.
T - Take frequent time-outs to reflect.
U - Utilize all resources before you make important decisions.
V - Visualize a goal and make steps toward the right direction.
X - Examine your motives.
Y - Yesterday is gone; tomorrow is not here, there is only today.
Z - Zero into being yourself not what other people want you to be.

A STUDENT IS A STUDENT

A student is a student
A learner or the same
Can be anyone, anywhere
With any particular name
A student is a student
A pupil who can tell
That it is important to study
Learn and excel

A student should be most of the following a b c's:

A - Attentive
B - Behaved
C - Considerate
D - Determined
E - Energetic
F - Flexible
G - Generous
H - Helpful
I - Inquisitive
J - Just
K - Knowledgeable
L - Loving
M - Mannerly
N - Notable
O - Optimistic
P - Punctual
Q - Quiet
R - Respectful
S - Studious
T - Truthful
U - Unique
V - Versatile
W - Watchful
X - Excited
Y - Yielding
Z – Zestfully cares about learning.

A student is a student
A learner or the same
Can be anyone, anywhere
With any particular name

WE'VE GOT PRIDE INSIDE

Stand up tall and get ready to shout
We've got pride from the inside out

      We've got pride inside!
      We've got pride inside!

We do our work in school each day
Our teachers want to show us the way

We've got pride inside!
We've got pride inside!

Being courteous and kind at any rate
Will help us to learn and appreciate

      We've got pride inside!
      We've got pride inside!

We take the time to listen and learn
School pride is our main concern

      We've got pride inside!
      We've got pride inside!

GIVE ME ... AND I'LL BE SATISFIED

Give me school pride, school pride
And I'll be satisfied
Give me school pride, school pride
And I'll be satisfied
Give me school pride, school pride
And I'll be satisfied
And I'll be satisfied, today!

Give me self-control
And I'll be satisfied
Give me self-control
And I'll be satisfied
Give me self-control
And I'll be satisfied
And I'll be satisfied, today!

Give me harmony
And I'll be satisfied
Give me harmony
And I'll be satisfied
Give me harmony
And I'll be satisfied
And I'll be satisfied, today!

Give me understanding
And I'll be satisfied
Give me understanding
And I'll be satisfied
Give me understanding
And I'll be satisfied
And I'll be satisfied, today!

Give me an education
And I'll be satisfied
Give me an education
And I'll be satisfied
Give me an education
And I'll be satisfied, and I'll be satisfied, today!

TO GET OVER, GET BETTER

To get over, get better!
To get over, get better!

Get better in reading
Get better in math
Have better comprehension
Stay on the right path
Get better in phonics
And spelling, too
Work really hard
Whatever you do!
Get better in science
In history, and gym
Study longer for tests
Don't rely on your whims
Get better at listening
Doing homework and more
Start answering more questions
To increase your scores
Have better conduct
Use more self-control
Be determined to get-
On the honor roll
Respect your teachers
Do better work
Complete your assignments
And don't act berserk
To be a good student
Takes practice each day
To get over, get better
Start now, today!

BUILDING SELF-CONFIDENCE

Building self-confidence
Is like building pride
It helps a person
Grow from inside

Building self-confidence
Is expressing praise
For an adult or child
In small simple ways

Building self-confidence
Is finding a person unique
When certain skills and qualities
Are good to uncover or seek

Building self-confidence
Is building self worth
And other strong abilities
Important to people on earth

Building self-confidence
Goes a very long way
In promoting positive feelings
Each and everyday

Building self-confidence
Improves confidence and more
It uplifts and enriches
By the score

Building self-confidence
Should be practiced each
day -
With parents and teachers
Leading the way

I AM SPECIAL

I am Special.
I'm a single package wrapped so nice and neat.

I am Special.
I am one of a kind that won't be made again.

I am Special.
My light is warm and reaches out for acceptance.

I am Special.
I listen and hear through my own limited scope.

I am Special.
Laughter is the melody of my soul.

I am Special.
Tears release my doubts and fears.

I am Special.
Take time to know me; let me fit into your world.

I am Special.
I have the power to soar if you let me be myself.

I am Special.
Try not to tear at the corners of my heart.

I am Special.
I have to try hard to do a little bit well.

I am Special.
Please give me forward praise rather than backward reminders.

I am Special.
Sometimes, when you see me look confused, remember that I am trying to bring order to a complex world.

I am Special.
When you scream at me, my feelings are hurt and I curl up tight inside.

I am Special.

I may appear slow and unyielding at times, but a bit of encouragement motivates me to do better.

I am Special.
Help comfort me because I haven't been loved very often or well.

I am Special.
I'm an important and necessary part of this world.

I am Special.
If by chance we meet on this horizon or at another time or place, lets link hearts, join hands, and share joys.

I am Special.
We can make a difference in each other's world.

I am Special.
Stand back, and watch me grow into something beautiful!

GIVE ME P-R-I-D-E

Give me a "P" - P- stands for Patience.
I must be patient and wait my turn.
It's a better way to listen.
It's a better way to learn.

Give me a "R" - R- stands for Respect.
I must respect my classmates and my friends.
I must realize that-
Together, we can blend.

Give me an "I" - I- stands for Interest.
I must show an interest in my studies at school.
I must pay attention and follow the rules.

Give me a "D" - D- stands for Determination.
I must be determined to get things done,
so I can be a help to everyone.

Give me an "E" - E- stands for Effort.
I must make an effort to do the best I can.
I have to study hard because my skills go hand in
hand.

What does it spell?
It spells PRIDE.
What does it spell?
It spells PRIDE?

Give me a P-R-I-D-E
Pride is a part of me
It is as easy to say as 1-2-3
Pride is a part of me
It is as easy to say as 1-2-3

I AM A LIGHT TO THE WORLD

I am a light to the world
Shining brightly for all to see
Just how marvelous I can be

I am a light to the world
My light reaches out far
Beyond the clouds, the sun, and stars

I am a light to the world
I have a soft warm glow
That radiates around those I know

I am a light to the world
I have many faces
I can live in a variety of places

I am a light to the world
I speak many languages and words
I need to be heard

I am a light to the world
I come in different shades
I approach life unafraid

I am a light to the world
To the world, to the world
I am a light to the world

WE MUST BE BETTER STUDENTS ONE AND ALL

To answer the call, we must be better students one and all.
To answer the call, we must be better students one and all.

To answer the call, our personal quest
Is to practice this alphabet and always do our best.

A- I <u>abide</u> by the rule that honesty is cool.
B- I <u>believe</u> that I can achieve.
C- <u>Capable</u> of success, I will do my best.
D- I will <u>decide</u> to carry myself with pride.
E- <u>Education</u> is the key to opportunity.
F- I can be <u>fair</u> and treat others with care.
G- I can be <u>good</u> the way that I should.
H- I must <u>hear</u> with an attentive ear.
I- I will <u>improve</u> and forward move.
J- I won't <u>judge</u> or hold a grudge.
K- To be <u>kind</u> is important to keep in mind.
L- <u>Listening</u> in school is a valuable tool.
M- I won't be <u>mean</u> or act nasty in between.
N- I <u>need</u> to take the time to read.
O- I will <u>obey</u> each and everyday.
P- I <u>plan</u> to do the best that I can.
Q- I will <u>quell</u> my urge to fight or yell.
R- I must <u>read</u> in order to succeed.
S- I can <u>study</u> with my good buddy.
T- I will watch my <u>temper</u> so I won't whine or whimper.
U- I <u>understand</u> that my skills go hand in hand.
V- I <u>vow</u> to do more than I ever did before.
W- I will <u>watch</u> what I say at home, at school and at play.
X- I will <u>examine</u> my mood and try not to be rude.
Y- I will <u>yield</u> better grades and look at the progress I have made.
Z- I can <u>zero</u> into school and follow all the rules.

To be better students, we must practice these a b c's
And, then we must act accordingly!

MAKE YOUR GOAL THE HONOR ROLL

Make your goal the Honor Roll
Make better grades to show the progress you have made
Listen to your teacher well
So that you won't fail
Improve your behavior each day,
By being courteous and kind along the way

On your Report card are letter grades
Each one reflects the growth you have made

An "A"- means "Excellent" and out of sight. It shows that you have been working with all of your might.

A "B"- means that you have been doing "Good", on a lot of your work the way that you should.

A "C"- means "Satisfactory", you have made it through but there is still more that you can do.

A "D"- means "Needs Improvement" all around. You better get your skills on more solid ground.

A "F"- means "Unsatisfactory". You have failed through and through on most of the work you were supposed to do.

You must be responsible and obey all the rules
To be a successful student in school

Come prepared to work and be on time
Be committed to learning without reasons or rhymes

Practice reading at home and do your spelling and math-
Because achieving in school keeps you on the right path!

I —— CAN —— MAKE —— IT

My life is before me
Is it all that it should be?
The world will get rough
I have to be tough
I can't be afraid
My plans must be made
From beginning to end
I must make amends

           Yes, I know right here and now that I can succeed
           Just to believe that I can is all that I need

I know that I <u>want</u> to make it.
I know that I <u>need</u> to make it.
I know that I <u>have</u> to make it.
My dreams go on and on and on and on and on.

I'll give it all that I can
And, courageously I will stand
Yet, I know that this time
I won't need any reasons or rhymes
So hold out your hand
Guide me across this great land
Because I want to do well
Beyond all things, excel

           Yes, I know right here and now that I can succeed
           Just to believe that I can is all that I need

I know that I <u>want</u> to make it.
I know that I <u>need</u> to make it.
I know that I <u>have</u> to make it.
My dreams go on and on and on and on and on.

136

THE 3 LITTLE " C's " ARE A PART OF ME

The 3 little "C's" are a part of me
A part of me, a part of me
The 3 little "C's" are a part of me
They are a part of me each day

The 3 little "C's" are: CARE, CALM and CONTROL.
CARE, CALM and CONTROL.
CARE, CALM and CONTROL.

The 3 little "C's" are: CARE, CALM and CONTROL.
The 3 little "C's" are a part of me.

I must "C" - number 1
To CARE about others
To CARE about others
To CARE about others
I must "C" - number 1
To CARE about others
In what I do and say

I must "C" - number 2
To always be CALM
To always be CALM
To always be CALM
I must "C" - number 2
To always be CALM
In what I do and say

I must "C" - number 3
To be in CONTROL
To be in CONTROL
To be in CONTROL
I must "C" - number 3
To be in CONTROL
In what I do and say

BUILDING BLOCKS THAT MAKE A BETTER STUDENT

There are building blocks to make a better student
They make a better student in school today

There are building blocks to make a better student
There are building blocks that pave the way

Block A- for ATTITUDE and ATTENTION
Block B- for BELIEF and BETTERMENT
Block C- for CARE and CONSIDERATION
Block D- for DRIVE and DETERMINATION
Block E- for EFFORT and ENTHUSIASM
Block F- for FORTITUDE and FLEXIBILITY
Block G- for GROWTH and GENEROSITY
Block H- for HAPPINESS and HELPFULNESS
Block I- for INTEREST and IMPROVEMENT
Block J- for JOBS and JUSTICE
Block K- for KINDNESS and KNOWLEDGE
Block L- for LISTENING and LEARNING
Block M- for MASTERY and MOTIVATION
Block N- for NEATNESS and NICENESS
Block O- for OPTIMISM and ORDERLINESS
Block P- for PATIENCE and PUNCTUALITY
Block Q- for QUIETNESS and QUALITY
Block R- for RESPECTFULNESS and RESPONSIBILITY
Block S- for SELF-ESTEEM and SELF-CONTROL
Block T- for TRUST and THOUGHTFULNESS
Block U- for UNDERSTANDING and USEFULNESS
Block V- for VIGOR and VITALITY
Block W- for WISDOM and WORTHINESS
Block X- for EXACTNESS and EXAMINATION
Block Y- for YIELDING and YEARNING
Block Z- for ZEST and ZEROING into goals and objectives.

There are building blocks that make a better student
That will make a better student from a to z

There are building blocks that make a better student
That stress good traits and qualities

138

ATTENDANCE MATTERS

Attendance Matters
It matters a lot
You have to be in school
To give it the best shot

Attendance Matters
With each day that you come
An important lesson is learned
A small victory is won

Attendance Matters
The days will appear
On your report card
And recorded throughout the year

Attendance Matters
It is as important as your grades
It gives a clear indication
Of the effort you have made

Attendance Matters
From the first day of school
To the end of the semester
Make perfect attendance the rule!

OH, GIVE ME A SCHOOL

Oh, give me a school
That will give me the tools
To succeed in this challenging world
There is so much to learn
I must show some concern
By practicing skills everyday

       Oh, I love my school
       I need to abide by the rules
       I'll be at school everyday
       Teachers will show me the way
       To a future both sound and secure

Oh, give me a school
That has consistent, firm rules
That I can follow each day
I must learn to read well
And work hard to excel
So I can be proud of myself

       Oh, I love my school
       It helps me learn valuable tools
       Like reading and math
       And to stay on the right path
       To a future both sound and secure

I CAN BE ANYTHING I WANT TO BE

I can be, I can be anything I want to be

I can be a doctor
I can be a nurse
I can be a poet
And, write a beautiful verse

I can be a lawyer
I can be a clerk
I can be a musician
Many places I can work

I can be a manager
And own my own store
I can be a policeman
All of these jobs and more

I can be a mechanic
Or, an astronaut, too
There are so many things
That I can do

I can be a teacher
And teach children how to read
Or, I can be a counselor
Helping people in need

I can be a carpenter
Making things out of wood
I can be a barber
I need practice to be good

I can be a beautician
And style a person's hair
Or, a flight attendant
Traveling here or there

I can be a typist
Typing at incredible speed
I can be a dentist
Education is what I need

20 CANS OF SUCCESS
20 CANS OF SUCCESS
CANS THAT CAN SUCCEED BEYOND ALL THE REST

1. I can do things well so that I can excel.
2. I can act right and not curse or fight.
3. I can read in order to succeed.
4. I can do more to increase my scores.
5. I can work and not go berserk.
6. I can speak out without having to shout.
7. I can be nice and listen to advice.
8. I can stand tall and get up after a fall.
9. I can wait without having to debate.
10. I can be strong and not do something wrong.
11. I can take turns without major concerns.
12. I can never take drugs or hang with thugs.
13. I can think and see, positively.
14. I can have fun without using a gun.
15. I can follow the rules and not act a fool.
16. I can be polite, morning, noon, or night.
17. I can use good manners without displaying some banners.
18. I can be on time without reasons or rhymes.
19. I can calm down and turn my life around.
20. I can be in control and get on the Honor Roll.

WITH 20 CANS OF SUCCESS
I CAN BE THE BEST!

The flowers that bloom in the mind are different from the garden kind
    The blossoms sprout from within,
        Without the aid of water or wind

The branches stem from keen insight and show a gradual degree of height
    The roots of wisdom are anchored deep,
        Where consciousness never sleeps

And buds stem internally, encompassing certain qualities
    Buds of compassion grow near,
        When sympathy and love appear

Honesty has flowers, too, with truth and justice shining through
    Trustworthiness is indeed a flower-
        That develops after thoughtful hours

And integrity springs anew with a code of character filtering through
    Self-discipline blooms as well,
        With sincerity enough to tell

Perseverance will take root when determination is clothed to suit
    Patience can grow gradually -
        When petals of knowledge are flowing free

A glimpse of what you internally grow is reflected in your deeds that show
    Take time to caress your inward flowers-
        With positive thoughts building strong, firm towers.

CHAPTER VI.

MATTERS
OF THE HEART

In Chapter VI the heart is symbolic; it is the place where love and peace preside. We need to get to the heart of the matter in teaching our children to be more compassionate. In communicating and generating a spirit of peace and harmony, we need to recognize the similarities, rather than the differences in people. In short, children need to look at others from the inside out.

* Teachers and parents can encourage children to be more loving and compassionate. They can be taught to express themselves in non-violent ways. The poems presented in this chapter are meant to uplift and inspire.

* Some examples of this are, 'The Language of the Heart', 'My Words Have Wings', and 'A Healthy Heart Beats Love'. Lessons can be based on 'Together We Can Make a Better World' and 'Beat the Heat' using current events, facts or features in history or in conjunction with a social studies curriculum or unit.

* The last selection entitled, 'Creative Activities' list a variety of activities that may actively engage learners.

147

*   A decorative addition to some of the poems or rhymes presented in this book could be to use poster boards, sentence strips or colored paper to make banners or charts to represent positive themes.

*   Pupil Pledge buttons could be made and worn to foster unity.

*   It is always a good idea to have Anger Management Booklets to allow students to write about their thoughts and feelings, especially when they are angry.

*
    Each peaceful mode or measure can add to a more harmonious world for us all.

MY WORDS HAVE WINGS

My words have wings that carry my thoughts and feelings to others.
I think loving and kind thoughts.
I speak loving and kind words.

Using the following a b c's, positive words come easily:
A- Admire. I admire about you, your good qualities through and through.
B- Brotherhood. Isn't it good to have a feeling of peace and brotherhood?
C- Cooperation. I cooperate with you, you cooperate with me; it's a wonderful world when we act peacefully.
D- Dignity. Dignity and pride go hand in hand besides.
E- Encouragement. Encouragement and trust are a definite must.
F- Feelings. I respect your feelings, I respect what you say; we need to talk politely to be heard each day.
G- Gentleness. A gentle approach is best whatever the deed, whatever the quest.
H- Harmony. Harmony is getting along like singing together a melody or song.
I- Improvement. Improvement can be great, for anyone at any rate.
J- Join. Let's join forces together, whatever the time, whatever the weather.
K- Kindness. Keeping kindness around is better I have found.
L- Love. Love is the key to dissolve hate and hostility.
M- Manners. Keep your manners uptight and always be polite.
N- Nice. Being agreeable and nice is like showing favor twice.
O- Optimistic. Being optimistic and bright helps problems turn out right.
P- Patience. Patience is the way to delay your wishes for another day.
Q- Quiet. Quiet and free of noise is a good way to study for girls and boys.
R- Respect. Respect is showing concern for other's feelings from which we can learn.
S- Secure. Free from fear, anxiety, or doubt is what the word secure is about.
T- Tenderness. Showing tenderness is best when it is followed by a warm caress.
U- Unity. Unity is a word that can unite to be heard.
V- Value. We all have value; we all have worth, living together on this earth.
W- Watch. Watch the words you think and say; make them positive everyday.
X- Examine. Examine how you speak and feel. Use words that help and heal.
Y- Yield. Learn to yield and with new friendships, build.
Z- Zero. Zero into kindness in thought and word today, and circulate good feelings along the way.

BEAT THE HEAT

Beat the heat of ANGER
Beat the fire of HATE
Enjoy life and living
Learn to appreciate

Beat the heat of VIOLENCE
Beat the sorrow and shame
Of hurting others
Or by calling people names

Beat the heat of HOSTILITY
Beat the need to FIGHT
There are better ways
To solve problems right

Beat the lack of TOLERANCE
Beat the lack of DISCIPLINE, too
Improve these features
Whatever you do

Beat the urge to be NASTY
Beat the urge to be MEAN
With all of the negative
Things in between

Beat HOT TEMPERS
Beat IMPATIENCE, today
Take the TIME and CHOOSE
The most CIVIL WAY!

THE LANGUAGE OF THE HEART

If you listen, you will hear the language of the heart.
Soft whispers speak in hushed tones.
It is a language of LOVE.
It is a language of PEACE.
It is a language of PURPOSE.

If you listen, you will hear the language of the heart.
Soft melodies linger in the wind.
It is a language of WISDOM.
It is a language of JOY.
It is a language of UNDERSTANDING.

If you listen, you will hear the language of the heart.
Soft notes are strumming tender songs.
It is a language of LIGHT.
It is a language of KINDNESS.
It is a language of ENCOURAGEMENT.

If you listen, you will hear the language of the heart.
Soft gentle words flow like water in a stream.
It is a language of BEAUTY.
It is a language of ACCEPTANCE.
It is a language of APPRECIATION.

If you listen, you will hear the language of the heart.
Try to feel the music.
Try to understand the words.
Try to interpret the message.
Try to move with the beat.

The language of the heart is an unspoken feeling that takes root and grows into
a symphony of love. The language of the heart speaks volumes from the depths
of your being. Take time to listen and hear.

YOU MAKE YOUR OWN WORLD

You make your own world

If you fight to solve problems, your world will be in chaos

You make your own world

If you always criticize or belittle others, your world will be without friends

You make your own world

If you constantly argue and disagree, your world will be lonely

You make your own world

If hate is a priority, your world will be without love

You make your own world

If you harbor jealously and envy, your world will be full of anxiety and doubt

You make your own world

If you fear failure or defeat, your world will show lack and limitation

You make your own world

Have a plan to follow.
Have goals to achieve.

POINTS TO PONDER

Use words that help not hurt.
Talk calmly without anger.

Practice being peaceful.
Practice being patient.
Practice being polite.

Don't be threatened by fear, change, or challenge.

You can't change anyone else but yourself.

Give the best gift of all: unselfish love.

Talk things over don't hold onto hate.

You don't need permission to change your mind or attitude.

Don't copy others. Be your own original.

Stay cool, calm, and in control.

Focus on forgiving yourself and others.

Disagree ... positively.

Stand back from anger before it stands for you.

Cursing and cussing won't gain respect.

Don't let hate circulate.

Sharing and caring give life purpose.

Form a bridge of love not a gate of hate.

Let your mind and body work as a team.

Write down mean, angry words on paper, not on the canvas of your mind.

If you force life to go your way, you may miss beautiful people, places, or things.
Don't focus on differences: welcome diversity.

A HEALTHY HEART BEATS LOVE

A healthy heart beats LOVE.
A healthy heart beats LOVE.
It's what the world needs more of.

To keep the heart healthy you must:
1. Avoid hate and hostility.
2. Control anger.
3. Stop negative thinking.
4. Avoid toxic people.
5. Reduce doubts and fears.
6. Exercise feelings of love, peace, and brotherhood.
7. Choose to be happy and upbeat.
8. Increase gifts and giving.
9. Decrease finding fault or blame.
10. Improve your attitude and behavior.
11. Continue good deeds and favors.
12. Practice doing the right thing.
13. Avoid excess worry and stress.
14. Listen with an understanding ear and heart.
15. Respond to others in need.
16. Discuss don't demand.
17. Go with a positive flow.
18. Stop bad habits.
19. Take time to enjoy life and living.
20. Have regular heart to heart talks with the ones you love.

A healthy heart beats LOVE.
A healthy heart beats LOVE.
It's what the world needs more of.

The first thing you see is the color of someone's skin but stop to look at the beauty within.

As long as there is a heart to heart connection going on, a thread of hope can follow along.

You can't stand not to be special because you are one of a kind.

Take time to learn something special about someone else.

An important part of learning is being able to appreciate the process.

Life is an education in learning about oneself.

Every change or challenge is a learning experience toward higher good.

Stop destructive behavior like hate and hostility.

Step by step, day by day, a positive thought helps pave the way.

Let hate ... evaporate.

Work on being more tolerant of other's thoughts, feelings, and opinions.

Exercise and practice more self-control.

A smile is like a ray of sunshine you can wear and share.

You can be nice not negative.

Better things happen with a better you!

THE WORLD

The world is round, yet the people I've found -

Don't live in PEACE and GOODWILL.

If only I could, I'd change things for good and label it BROTHERHOOD!

SO ... THE CYCLE GOES

As morning is to day and night
So the cycle goes my friend, so the cycle goes

Stay in school and do what's right
So the cycle goes my friend, so the cycle goes

Stop the fighting here and now
So the cycle goes my friend, so the cycle goes

It is better to love anyhow
So the cycle goes my friend, so the cycle goes

Stop the violence everywhere
So the cycle goes my friend, so the cycle goes

Let's make an effort to help and care
So the cycle goes my friend, so the cycle goes

Let's show how we can get along
So the cycle goes my friend, so the cycle goes

Then we can sing a peaceful song
So the cycle goes my friend, so the cycle goes

STOP THE CYCLE OF VIOLENCE
START A CYCLE OF PEACE
STOP THE CYCLE OF HATE
LET THE KILLINGS CEASE!

TOGETHER WE CAN MAKE A BETTER WORLD

Together we can make a better world.
Together, together, together
We can make a better world.
What can we do to make a better world?

Together we can:
> Stop fighting,
> Focus on Peace,
> Be Courteous,
> Use Good Manners,
> Be Compassionate,
> Treat people Kindly,
> Help instead of Hurting,
> Share and Take Turns,
> Respect all Living Creatures,
> Play Fair,
> Celebrate Diversity,
> Obey your Parents and Teachers,
> Stop Bad Habits,
> Have a Positive Attitude,
> Don't Use Profanity,
> Speak in a Calm Manner,
> Don't Litter,
> Protect the Environment,
> Handle Problems Peacefully,
> Forgive and Forget past infractions
> > And,
> Remember to allow for Individual Differences in Thought, Word, and Deed.

CREATIVE ACTIVITIES

1. <u>Read Books and Different Newspapers.</u> Pretend you are an editor or reporter. Write your own version of an accident, event, or newsworthy item.

2. <u>Coordinate Events.</u> Imagine planning daily, weekly, or monthly activities for a particular group of people. Research different cultures, customs, and countries.

3. <u>Examine Medical Books or Journals.</u> Construct models of the human body. Match diseases with known causes and cures.

4. <u>Collect Automobile Ads from Magazines or Newspapers.</u> Develop new ways to market or sell the cars of the future.

5. <u>Write Your Own Television or Radio Show.</u> Develop topics and terms that focus on current issues and different points of view. Practice performing live and on tape.

6. <u>Study Sign Language.</u> Practice communicating in sign language.

7. <u>Collect Comic Books.</u> Write your own comics or cartoons. Make a television screen to show your action packed pictures.

8. <u>Tackle the Problems of World Peace.</u> Develop methods to promote peace in the world. Gather articles about disasters or terrorism. Construct plans to deal with emergencies. Develop a Peace Plan to reduce violence locally and internationally.

9. <u>Research Your Family Tree.</u> Ask questions and take notes when talking to relatives. View and study a family album or archive.

10. <u>Create a Time Capsule.</u> Collect items to portray life as it is now. Write detailed information about people, places, and things.

11. <u>Focus On Gang Prevention.</u> Establish programs and create slogans. Make posters to highlight anti- gang messages and themes.

12. <u>Start Your Own Business.</u> Learn how to get a business started from the ground up. Think about the people you would serve and the products that you would need.

13. **Form a People's Court.** Learn court procedures and study laws. Research past and present court cases in the news.

14. **Plan a Career Workshop.** Discuss and list the negative and positive aspects of certain jobs or professions.

15. **Form a Friendship Club.** Match people and interests together. Evaluate what makes friendship important. List qualities that you like about yourself and others. Make friendship necklaces, bracelets, and tokens.

16. **Prepare a Museum Exhibit.** Gather materials and items to display. Write interesting details about your exhibit. Research important facts and features.

17. **Make an Animal Habitat.** Construct a dwelling for animals. Use common objects found in the home or from nature.

18. **Write a Screenplay for a Movie.** Focus on solving social issues or problems. Study film- making and production.

19. **Start A Recycling Program.** Write slogans to improve the recycling efforts in your community. Organize a recycling campaign.

20. **Make a Comical Cookbook.** Collect recipes and cookbooks. Substitute funny or imaginary ingredients for common ones.

21. **Draw Treasure Maps.** Study an atlas, map, or globe. Think about streets, buildings, lakes, rivers, and points of interest. Make the treasure map fun and interesting.

22. **Compare Cereal Boxes.** List ingredients from boxes of cereal or other containers of food. Look up unfamiliar words in the dictionary. Study vitamins, minerals, and food groups.

23. **Sew a Rug or Quilt.** Gather scraps of material from a variety of sources. Sew pieces together around a central theme or idea.

24. **Trace Common Objects To Form a Shape Collage.** Select items around the house and trace them on paper. Disguise the drawings with different colors and designs.

25. **Make an Herb Garden.** Study different herbs and seasonings. Make a window herb garden. List herbs and seasonings found in your home.

Conclusion

Violence hampers the thinking and reasoning of our youth and may destroy precious moments of childhood. Images of violence and destruction fill the minds and hearts of many of our children. Don't Fight, Forgive is a book that attempts to counteract some of the violence in our society through the use of poetry, morals, and messages.

All children have power and potential and this resource should not be wasted on violent acts and deeds. We must intervene in the thoughts, feelings, and emotions of our children. We must help them build blocks of good behavior on a foundation of love and respect. We must connect with our youth and redirect their negative habits and thinking. Our children must be encouraged to discuss their pains and problems openly and freely. They must be taught peaceful and civil ways of solving their disagreements.

We as parents and teachers must listen with an understanding heart and ear to what concerns our youth and their world. Likewise, we must teach and demonstrate socially acceptable methods of communicating wants and needs. These standards of behaving in an acceptable manner must be practiced on a regular basis, so that they become an integral part of everyday life. In short, we must set rules of behavior for our children to live by and follow.

Peace is an attainable goal. We should all be involved in building bridges of love not gates of hate. We are raising children in difficult times. We must take responsibility for putting into place the morals and manners they will need to succeed in the future. Together, we can make a peaceful world.

Judith GrandPre' Smith is a Special Education teacher with the Chicago Public School System. She is a poet, musician, and artist who has had works displayed at art fairs and museums throughout the city. She is actively involved in programs that emphasize the arts for children and young adults.

Judith is a poet for many reasons and seasons. She writes poetry for retirement parties, birthdays, weddings, and other special occasions. She is also the author of the motivational poetry book, <u>Light Up Learning</u> and three posters entitled, "Someday", "We Are The True Americans", and "Ebony Woman".

Mrs.Smith has received various notable awards. In 1992, she received the Professional Literacy Achievement Award from the American Association of University Women, and in 1993, the Department of Special Education award from Chicago State University. Several grants awarded to her include a Chicago Foundation of Education Small Grant in 1998, and The Rochelle Lee Fund Grant in 2001. Additionally, a Target for Teachers Scholarship was awarded to her in 2000 for promoting anti-violence programs in the community. Mrs. Smith is also a Teacher Consultant for the Chicago Area Writing Project at Roosevelt University.

The major area of focus for Judith Smith is in violence prevention and character education programs for children. She is developing a teacher's guide for educators to use to incorporate anti-violence poetry, stories, slogans, and themes throughout the curriculum.